Jay —

An excellent +

first meeting — +

look forward to

knowing you better.

Best

[signature]

2/18/04

PIPES

The CEO's Guide to Successful
Private Investments in Public Equities

PIPES

Harlan P. Kleiman
Ronald F. Richards

PARACHUTE
BUSINESS PRESS

San Francisco • 2003

PIPES

Book designed by
Paula Doubleday Design Inc.

www.parachutebusinesspress.com

Library of Congress Cataloging-in-Publication
Data available.

ISBN: 0-9726623-0-8

Printed in Canada

Table of Contents

Acknowledgments

We would like to thank the team members, present and past, at Shoreline Pacific, LLC for their valuable contributions to this book: Nina Cartee, Jane Clifford, Matthew Close, Andrea Goldman, Marie Jorajuria, Linda Kosut, Vida Buchalter Harband, and Katherine Winkler.

We would also like to thank our wives, Sandy Kleiman and Jill Richards, for their continued support and encouragement throughout the process of writing this book—we could not have completed *PIPES* without them.

Introduction

A Monday in October 1987. My company had just been authorized to do a public offering the Friday before and I was flying from Los Angeles to New York to begin an investor road show. If all went right, we would be public and financed in the next sixty days. The market, however, was under terrible pressure, and within the five hours it took to fly from LAX to New York the NASDAQ dropped 500 points. To call my IPO dead would be putting a positive spin on it. I called my underwriter who, if this were 1929, would probably have jumped from his office window. He was wiped out and so was my financing.

I couldn't accept this. I told myself I would live to see another day. I would get my company public by sheer dint of will. The good news was that I eventually did. The bad news was that I had to give up too much for too little money, and I *still* didn't have enough cash to fulfill my business strategy. I now had an undercapitalized public company in a capital-intensive business that was in jeopardy from day one much because it needed more capital to survive and grow.

I talked with a slew of investment bankers. "I want to do a private financing," I told them. "I want to know who my next round of investors are—I need to show them where I'm taking this company." "Great plan, but it's too soon to do a follow on," the investment bankers told me. "I don't want to do a follow on," I told them, "I want to do a private placement." "But you're a public company," they said. "A private placement can't be done, not yet—it would show weakness. It will kill your company."

The only people who would listen to me were the "predatory bottom-fishers" with no creative ideas and no relationships with the kind of investors I wanted in my company. So in order to grow, I took chances. I committed to transactions that were less than prudent. And I watched my company collapse.

When I stopped cursing the dark and did a postmortem, I concluded that a good business strategy could easily be killed not only by lack of capital, but also by lack of *knowledgeable* and *responsible* capital. I decided to create a firm to provide private strategic investments in public companies.

That was 72 companies and over $1.5 billion ago. Shoreline Pacific (by this or its former names) is now twelve years old. Its PIPE (private investments in public equities) transactions have been responsible for the survival and growth of countless public companies that probably would have perished had this form of financing not been available. And all of this was accomplished during a time when PIPEs had a reputation as "toxic" or the investment vehicle of last resort.

Have PIPEs been abused? Absolutely. But every financial instrument has been abused, especially when they are first introduced and regulatory agencies have not yet created guidelines. When properly constructed and executed, PIPEs are fast, discreet, and can be tailored to meet each company's needs. They improve institutional ownership, increase liquidity, reduce financial costs, and are generally more precise and certain than almost any public offering.

Now for the most interesting part of all: recently, as public offerings have become difficult to conclude, bulge-bracket investment banking firms have been recommending PIPEs as a mainstream form of financing. PIPEs are now everywhere!

But PIPEs have always been simply another financial instrument with characteristics that can be more or less effective than other financing vehicles, depending on a company's profile and the purpose of financing.

Hopefully this book will empower you to use PIPEs dynamically. Ron Richards and I believe we have barely scratched the surface of the creative utility of this tool.

Harlan P. Kleiman
Sausalito, California
January 2003

CHAPTER 1

OVERVIEW OF PIPES

W hen we talk with CEOs about private investments in public equities—PIPEs, for short—we try to accomplish two things. The first is to help them understand how PIPEs really work. The second is to help them assess PIPEs against other forms of financing available to their firm. Although facilitating PIPEs is our business— together we have structured more than 125 PIPE deals, ranging in size from a few million dollars to $375 million, approaching close to $1.8 billion in total financing—it is never our objective to convince a CEO that a PIPE is the best form of financing for their company. It is our desire that by the end of the conversation, the CEO understand PIPE financing relative to other forms of financing, with strengths and weaknesses that vary in every case depending on many things, including the particular strengths and weaknesses of their own company. And at that point, the CEO will be able to make an informed decision regarding the best form of financing for their firm.

In discussing PIPEs, we begin the conversation wherever the CEO wishes. Often, the starting point is a horror story about PIPEs that the CEO has read, while other times it is the urgent need the company has for cash. Sometimes, CEOs tell us they already know everything there is to know about PIPEs, but to talk to them anyway. In each case, we attempt to address the CEO's concerns in order to be certain they have a full understanding of where PIPEs fit into the full range of financing options.

In writing a book, it is always difficult to know the best place to begin the dialogue so that the reader's burning questions are quickly addressed. Perhaps the most notable thing about PIPEs is their conflicting reputation as both an excellent way to raise money quickly, and a dangerous financing tool that can send a company into a "death spiral"—hence the nickname *toxic* and the notion that PIPEs are strictly a financing vehicle of "last resort." How can both be true? This paradox is heightened by the fact that PIPEs are an increasingly popular and by now an accepted, mainstream form of financing.

PIPEs can take many different forms,
including common stock, common stock
and warrants, convertible preferred stock,
convertible debt, and equity lines.

We will begin with this paradox as a way of addressing the many questions and concerns you have about PIPEs. Our goal is to help you feel certain you are making the best possible decision as to whether a PIPE is right for your firm—and if so what kind of PIPE—so that you can move forward confidently into what may seem like foreign territory. We've laid out the book as follows:

- In this opening chapter, we'll give an overview of PIPEs, including basic definitions, advantages and disadvantages, trends, potential considerations, and some popular myths.

- In Chapter 2, we'll cover the two basic frameworks of a PIPE deal.

- In Chapters 3 and 4, we'll talk about the specific types of securities available for use within particular PIPE frameworks. We'll then describe the types of features that you should be considering for these securities.

- In Chapter 5, our final chapter, we'll show you how to use what you've learned to assemble a team of financial and legal advisors that will put together the best possible PIPE for your unique circumstances. This will include the types of questions you should be asking to make sure members of your deal team really know their PIPEs and aren't simply learning at your expense.

What Is a PIPE?

Let's get started by defining our terms. *Private investments in public equity,* commonly referred to as PIPEs, are privately negotiated sales of a public company's securities. In practice, the securities are usually sold to institutional investors. They are generally sold through an exemption in the securities laws and therefore cannot be resold into the public market until a registration statement has been filed and declared effective or pursuant to an exemption under the securities laws. To compensate for this lack of immediate liquidity, PIPEs are often sold at a discount or structured to include other features that mitigate risk for the investor.

When public market funding was significantly curtailed in 2001, PIPE transactions considerably outpaced follow-on public offerings and became the funding vehicle of choice.

No two PIPEs are exactly alike. One of the most exciting things about working with PIPEs is that they are flexible and each is uniquely tailored to the particular circumstances involved. PIPEs can take many different forms, including common stock, common stock and warrants, convertible preferred stock, convertible debt, and structured private equity lines which are actually a hybrid of a PIPE and a public offering (all are discussed in Chapter 3). Like public offerings, PIPEs can range from very conservative to very aggressive. PIPEs are used to finance numerous activities, including growth capital, mezzanine funding, M&A financing, recapitalizations, as well as working capital and general corporate purposes.

The PIPEs market, virtually unknown until recently, has blossomed in the past few years. This can be seen by looking at the amount of money being raised, as well as at the number of PIPEs being completed, both in terms of deal structure and size. Since 1995, over 3,300 PIPEs of varying structures have been executed. When public market funding was significantly curtailed in 2001, PIPE transactions considerably outpaced follow-on public offerings and became the funding vehicle of choice.

Figure 1: Yearly PIPE Transactions 1995–2002

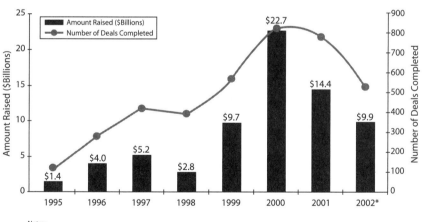

Notes:
Excludes OTC and Bulletin Board listed stocks. Excludes 144-A and Reg-S Deals.
*Estimated.

In short, PIPE financings have become accepted as a viable financing alternative for all types of public companies looking to raise money quickly and discreetly. One reason is that PIPEs can have numerous advantages for both the company and the investors. PIPEs can:

- Save time and money

- Add flexibility in financing

- Be completed discreetly

- Match companies with experienced investors that can be sources of more than just capital for the growth of the company

- Offer an alternative source of financing during times when the public markets are effectively "closed" for follow-on public offerings.

- Be individually tailored to fit the situation

When specifically compared to a public offering, PIPE transactions also have numerous advantages for both investors and public companies seeking to raise capital. Among the most important advantages are:

- **Less executive management time required.** Private transactions take significantly less senior management time than is required when doing a public offering. Lengthy roadshows in many cities are not necessary. Rather, an investment banker can match an issuer with a limited number of prescreened investors for direct due diligence and negotiations.

- **Less disruption to stock prices.** Because PIPE financing uses a controlled, private process, flexible terms can be quickly and discreetly negotiated, alleviating volatility fueled by market speculation.

- **Funding is expedited.** PIPE transactions are completed and the company can receive its funding before the securities are registered. In a public offering, the deal closes and the company gets its funding after the securities are registered. Therefore, the company can get its cash much faster with a PIPE than through a public transaction.

- **Investors execute definitive purchase agreements.** In a public offering, only indications of interest (so-called "circling") may occur prior to the time the registration statement is declared effective. A company cannot legally accept firm commitments to purchase from the investor until after the SEC declares the registration statement effective. The company therefore has no assurance that the time and money spent on preparing a registration statement and proceeding through the SEC review process will actually result in sales of its securities. In contrast, with a PIPE transaction an investor's obligation to purchase the agreed upon securities is executed before the company incurs time and expense filing a registration statement, significantly reducing the risk to the issuer that a financing will, in fact, take place and on what terms.

- **Reduced expenses.** The expense required to complete a PIPE can be substantially less than that needed to complete a public offering. Since a detailed prospectus need not be prepared and distributed to market the deal, there are tremendous cost savings in legal, accounting, and printing fees.

- **Structured to mitigate difficult market conditions.** PIPEs are negotiated transactions, allowing the parties to directly address company-specific issues, such as the impact of bad news, depressed stock price, low volume, or significant uncertainty regarding the company's future.

- **Ability to incorporate future valuation events.** PIPE transactions can take into account anticipated future valuation events such as FDA approvals, alliances, or new product introductions, through the use of price adjustment mechanisms.

What Is a Death Spiral?

If PIPEs have so many good features, why are they controversial? The greatest concern CEOs have about PIPEs is that they will result in excessive dilution of the company's stock in the market. As a result of bad press and losses related to bad deals, some CEOs are adamantly opposed to PIPE deals.[1] How realistic are these fears?

---

[1] At least one institutional investor goes to great lengths to prevent its portfolio companies from engaging in PIPE deals, including writing to companies threatening lawsuits if they take on PIPE financing, selling their investments in such companies, adding provisions to their investment documents to prohibit convertible deals, and threatening to pull its business from investment banks engaged in PIPEs.

The greatest concern CEOs have about PIPEs is that they will result in excessive dilution of their company's stock.

In talking with CEOs, we take significant care to discuss how certain types of investors can misuse PIPEs, and describe the simple steps they can take to protect their company from harm. The terms *toxic* and *death spiral* stem from a form of convertible PIPEs used for high-risk investments where investors require significant downside protection. In the worst-case scenario, this type of PIPE can cause massive dilution of the company's stock and the potential delisting of the company in the public market as a result of a significant decline in its stock price. With conventional fixed-price convertibles, the conversion price is set in advance at the time of issuance. But in a death spiral scenario, the conversion price is set at the time of conversion, and moves up and down with the market. The cheaper the stock price, the more shares the investor obtains upon conversion of securities and the more dilution that occurs to existing holders. This mechanism protects the investor at the expense of the existing shareholders who bear the bear the dilution burden resulting from the issuance of additional shares.

Obviously, this feature can be abused by overly aggressive investors who by themselves can short the stock enough to depress the stock price and therefore benefit further as they receive more company stock upon conversion. It becomes a vicious cycle: the more shares that are sold, the lower the price goes, with the investor getting even more shares, adding additional pressure on the stock price. The descent can be dramatic. Several companies have suffered from such spirals and were never able to recover. These transactions are the exception, not the rule, and they can be avoided with careful advice and structuring—we'll talk more about this when we address the kinds of features you should build into a PIPE.

It is important to understand that convertible securities have often received misplaced blame for being the primary cause of a firm's financial collapse. However, companies that issue such convertible securities are often already troubled and therefore have no other acceptable alternatives for financing. In such situations, floating convertibles may be the *only* means of rescuing the business plan for the existing shareholders, short of declaring bankruptcy (in which case, common equity is typically wiped out because it stands behind all debt and preferred shares in priority).

When analyzing convertible securities transactions entered into by such companies, it is often difficult to separate fundamental flaws in the company's business model from stock trading activity in the market to identify the true cause of the declining stock price.

Consider as a case study the experience of Smith, Inc., an online business-to-business company that raised $50 million in a PIPE issuance of convertible preferred with a floating conversion rate. The company had been experiencing explosive sales growth and had a market cap at the time of $300 million. Despite an enormous run-up in revenues (to $15 million in their most recent quarter), there were signs that not all was well with its financial condition. During the quarter, their operating losses were more than twice their sales and interest expense almost 55 percent of gross profit. Capital expenditures that quarter rose to more than 150 percent of sales. While hoping that continued enormous growth of sales might actually save the company, Smith warned that their fourth quarter earnings would be off by as much as 50 percent. Although the company had entered into a floating price convertible without a floor—a death spiral—the company's financial results were so poor that it would be quite difficult to claim that the security—and not the company—caused it to declare bankruptcy two quarters later, less than a year after the PIPE was completed. The company chose a PIPE because it was quick and easy, and because they had limited options available to them since they didn't act earlier when they had alternatives. Was the PIPE responsible for Smith's demise? It's an oversimplification to say the PIPE was the primary cause when the company was riddled with business problems as well.

Now that we know the potential impact of significant dilution, how can we best avoid it? An issuer must be knowledgeable of, and insist upon having, certain beneficial provisions built into the transaction to protect the company and its shareholders. Dilution can be controlled: conversion caps and pricing floors can be incorporated into a PIPE structure to limit how low the convertible exercise price can adjust upon a decline in the stock price. These provisions and other important features are discussed in Chapter 4 of this book. But if we could boil it down to one rule of PIPEs, it would be as follows: *You should always avoid deals where the investor makes more money if the stock price goes down than if it appreciates.*

There are instances in which the company's state of affairs or market conditions are such that the only way for a company to get funding is through some form of convertible instrument purchased by an investor with a relatively short-term focus. In these cases, it may be reasonable for the investors to place the majority of the risk on the company. Company management needs to be aware of and understand what is reasonable. If the investor demands onerous terms, the cost to the company to acquire the necessary cash could, in the end, significantly harm the existing shareholders in the future. But most of the time, issuers have far more alternatives than they think. Unfortunately, they often wait to finance because they think their stock price is too low at the time and do not pursue financing until their cash reserves are too low. There is often little reason for the stock price to rise and they end up doing a transaction on far more onerous terms than would have been necessary if they had proactively pursued financing earlier.

Might a PIPE be the right choice for financing your firm? We're certainly not suggesting that PIPEs are right for all companies and all investors. We are saying that, *properly structured*, PIPEs can be highly beneficial to both parties. PIPEs are an efficient way to raise money and can be a very powerful financial tool when used properly.

Certainty in an Uncertain World

Whenever we talk with a CEO about doing a PIPE we like to walk through the following diagram (Figure 2). We call it *Certainty in an Uncertain World*. In it we have tried to capture some of the key variables to consider when deciding whether the best strategy is a public or a private offering.

You should always avoid deals where the investor makes more money if the stock price goes down than if it appreciates.

Figure 2: Certainty in an Uncertain World

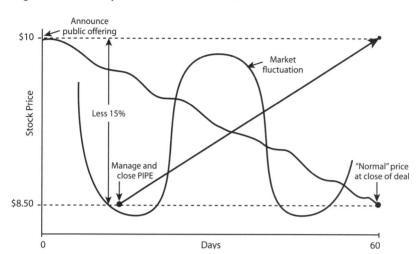

At first it might seem one of the strongly *negative* features of a PIPE is that you are selling stock at a discount of perhaps 10 to 15 percent of the publicly traded price. (We will cover the reasons why this discount is offered in the next chapter.) In the example given on our diagram, we have shown the PIPE price at $8.50 per share, compared to a publicly traded price at Day 1 of $10 per share. Naturally, if the choice were simply a matter of selling stock for $8.50 per share or selling it for $10 per share, the decision would not be difficult. After all, successful CEOs don't make a habit of giving away shareholder value by selling the company's stock at a price less than it is worth.

But it is important to compare apples to apples when deciding between PIPEs and public offerings. As with many things in life, timing is everything. A fundamental difference between PIPEs and follow-on public offerings involves when the market learns about the deal. With a PIPE, the market learns about the deal after it is already completed; in other words, the price has already been determined and the deal has closed when it is announced. With a public offering, the market learns of the pending deal when the registration statement is filed, but the price will not be determined until the deal closes, typically about 60 days later. Will that $10 per share really be there at Day 60 on our timeline? Typically, the stock price declines over the roughly 60 days between the follow-on public offering being announced and the stock actually being sold. If historical trends are any guide, this price dilution normally runs in the range of 10 to 15 percent. Given this line of reasoning, it might then seem obvious that doing a PIPE would be the best course. After all, it would seem better to get your $8.50 a share today rather than waiting 60 days to receive roughly the same amount of money.

But this, too, would be an oversimplification. The truth is that no one knows where the stock price will be in 60 days. And the number of variables that can influence its rise or fall are unlimited. They can include everything from company-specific issues (for example, missing an earnings estimate) to a general gain (or loss) in investor confidence in the market as a whole. In short, there are so many variables in play that no one can understand or compute the potential impact of all of them. In fact, this is very much the kind of atmosphere where analysis paralysis can set in.

Clearly, none of us can know the future. The best we can hope to do is to think logically about the factors that are within our control. As the chart shows, there is one big difference between PIPEs and public offerings: *when you get your money.* With a PIPE, you get your money quickly, and that means you can take action quickly too. As we all know in business, the phrase "time kills deals" often holds true. With PIPE financing, you can put the money to the desired use *before* the opportunity can fade away or die. In a world of uncertainty, PIPEs offer the critical advantage of providing your company with funding while the deal, the possibility, the future are all still alive. And because you have the money and can put it to work for you, the fears you may have regarding dilution may be offset by the positive steps you are taking to move your company forward. After all, it isn't ownership dilution that brings down the stock price, since most public investors are not focused on the exact percentage of the company that they own. Rather, it's dilution in the value of the company, and correspondingly its stock price, that hits investors where they live. If the proceeds of a PIPE offering can be used to improve the future prospects of the company and thereby increase its valuation, then you should probably do the deal and move forward.

Conclusion

In this chapter, we have tried to give you a general sense of what PIPEs involve and the considerations you need to keep in mind. Fundamentally, a PIPE is simply a form of financing with inherent advantages and disadvantages, like any other type of financing. Once you strip away all the scare tactics and rumors, you can dispassionately consider whether a PIPE is right for you in your particular situation. When armed with the proper information, you will see PIPEs simply as one more tool in your financial toolkit, something for you to take out and use when it is needed.

This concludes our overview of PIPEs. Figure 3 summarizes the structure of this book and also gives you a conceptual map for thinking about PIPEs. It's time now to get a better sense of what they actually involve, the framework of how they are created, and how your company might fit into that overall sense of structure. That's the focus of our next chapter.

Figure 3: A Conceptual PIPEs Map

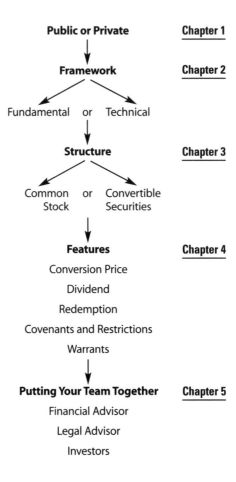

CHAPTER 2

THE PIPE FRAMEWORK

At this point, we have defined PIPEs and reviewed their relative advantages and potential disadvantages. In presenting this material (both in this book and when we deal with clients in our practice), our primary goals are to help company management assess their financing options and to ensure that they understand PIPEs before summarily dismissing them based on misconceptions. In particular, we seek to dispel two stereotypes: first, that PIPEs are only for companies in deep trouble, and second, that PIPEs are only for certain kinds of companies in particular niches and industries. Companies are often blinded by these stereotypes and completely miss the value of PIPEs as a financial tool that might be perfectly suited to their needs.

When talking with CEOs we underscore that there are four basic factors a company should look at when considering a PIPE transaction against a follow-on public offering:

- **Market environment.** At times, the market can be unreceptive to new stock issuances, such as in a recession or market downturn. In such instances, a company's public offering may not be well received, and therefore the company's chances for raising capital are better in the private equity market. Why? PIPE investors typically spend more time on company due diligence than those investing in public offerings. In a tough environment, a company may need the extended interaction to convince an investor to take part in the deal.

- **Timing.** A follow-on public offering generally takes approximately two to three months. Certain situations make it necessary for a company to raise capital more quickly, such as the need for additional working capital to complete a major project or funds to complete an acquisition, or simply the need for management to maintain its focus on the business rather than spending a great amount of time raising capital. PIPEs can facilitate the raising of funds quickly for whatever reason the funds are needed or desired.

PIPE can utilize any legitimate security structure
to allocate the risks of a transaction to the
appropriate party.

- **Fundamental issues.** Some public companies or market sectors are cyclical in nature, such as the life sciences industry. In such cases, Wall Street can be apathetic, making it difficult or imprudent for a company to raise money through a public offering. In these cases, PIPEs are a viable alternative to public transactions.

- **Special needs.** In some instances, companies have special needs and must negotiate unique terms with sophisticated investors, which are not available in a public transaction. For example, a biotech company about to achieve a significant milestone may want to sell stock at a premium today, but be willing to adjust the price if the milestone doesn't occur within a certain timeframe.

Besides the tendency of some CEOs to view PIPEs as emergency financing, there has also been the tendency to think of PIPEs as being appropriate only for smaller, cash-intensive, high-growth companies (for example, high-tech or biotech firms). In fact, PIPEs have become well-established alternative financing vehicles for a wide range of companies, including some larger, better capitalized, well-known firms. If you believe a PIPE might be worth exploring for your company, the next step is to consider the PIPE framework that would best meet your needs.

Shifting the Allocation of Risk

To help you consider the basic type of PIPE deal that might be best for your company, we have developed a model that divides PIPEs into two basic frameworks in accordance with how the PIPEs allocate risk. This model can help you not only to choose the appropriate PIPE framework for your company, but also can give you a sense of what you may need to do to restructure your company or reposition how your company is perceived by investors (through the type of story you tell to the investment community) in order to get the kind of deal you want.

PIPE investors, like all investors, are willing to take risks that are commensurate with the potential for returns from their invested capital: the higher the perceived risk, the higher the desired reward. The flexibility of PIPE financing enables investors to structure some of the risks out of the

In the case of a strong company or story, while investors might like features that provide downside protection they are not generally in a position to demand them.

transaction through a variety of mechanisms. The risk profile of the issuer and the return requirements of the investors will therefore drive the choice of PIPE framework, which can be broadly categorized as either *fundamental* or *technical*. What is the difference between the two? In a fundamental deal, almost all of the financial risk is placed squarely on the shoulders of the investor. In technical deals, some of the risks to the investor are shifted to the company and its existing shareholders. PIPEs can utilize any legitimate security structure to allocate the risks of a transaction to the appropriate party in order to meet the needs of both parties in the transaction. Let's now drill down further to get a better understanding of both fundamental and technical PIPEs.

Fundamental PIPE Deals

Fundamental deals refer to PIPEs where the investor is investing in the company on the basis of strong fundamentals. Fundamental investors do not require a high level of downside protection to convince them to invest in the company. In the case of a strong company or story, although investors might like features that provide downside protection, they are not generally in a position to demand them. If the demand is high enough for the company's securities, the company is in a position to stand its ground and not offer protective mechanisms.

What are strong fundamentals? Strong fundamentals can include financial performance, such as growing revenues and positive operating cash flows, but could just as easily include a strong concept or story that investors like at the time of the investment. (As an example, consider amazon.com at the time of its initial public offering: it had a strong, compelling story, even though it was generating significant losses.)

Other factors that support the pursuit of an attractive fundamental PIPE include:

- A strong, seasoned management team with relevant industry experience

- A detailed business plan with well-defined milestones

The company needs to be aware of and understand what allocation of risk is reasonable, and an expert advisor can assist the company with this evaluation.

- Significant growth potential, including:
  - Product or service with sufficient customer demand
  - Growing market with significant potential

One further note: in this section, we have stressed the strength of the company's story in accounting for fundamental deals, but another important reason that issuers want to use common stock is *simplicity*. The market understands common stock deals—they are easier to analyze and model. The mechanics of Wall Street are such that the easier a company is to understand, the more likely it is that analysts will take the effort to follow the company and write about it in their research. For these reasons—related more to human nature than to finance—companies may prefer to avoid complex securities on their balance sheet.

Technical PIPE Deals

Technical deals generally refer to convertible debt or convertible preferred stock, each of which are convertible into common stock. Technical deals are entered into for a variety of reasons. Some investors prefer to invest only in securities that have a higher priority upon liquidation than common stock and offer the investors other protections as well (for example, antidilution). In other cases, the company's fundamental outlook requires a security to be issued which has some protections for the investor that are not available when the security involved is common stock.

When a company's operating and financial fundamentals are not as strong, or the company's story is not compelling to investors, then investors will require additional protections for their temporarily illiquid investment in the PIPE. They will seek to shift some of the risks back to the company. Moreover, there are instances in which market conditions are such that the only way for a company to get funding is through some form of convertible instrument purchased by a relatively short-term investor. Depending on the circumstances, it may be reasonable for the investor to shift a significant amount of risk to the company. The company needs to be aware of and understand what allocation of risk is reasonable, and an expert advisor can assist the company with this evaluation. In

The technical investor will assess the overall riskiness of the investment based on the trading characteristics of the company's common stock.

certain situations, technical PIPEs are a viable, flexible financing alternative to the public markets, and can even be more appropriate than public financing. But with the burden of responsibility for success shifted to the company, the company must be comfortable that it understands the subtle nuances of the deal and the related implications of each.

The technical investor will assess the overall riskiness of the investment based primarily on the trading characteristics of the company's common stock. The more liquid the stock, the less protections an investor needs because the investor can exit the investment readily. The less liquid, the more protections from downturns the investor needs.

Downside protections to the investor can come in many forms. At the most basic level, the type of security selected can provide an element of protection. By using a convertible preferred or debt security, the investor is positioned higher in the capital structure than common stockholders and therefore has a preference in the event of liquidation (that is, the preferred shareholders get their money back before the common shareholders). In addition, a convertible security, by its nature, can incorporate additional features that are not typically associated with common equity. For example, features such as convertibility into common stock and preferred dividends. The most common protective feature is some form of adjustable conversion price. These types of features are discussed more fully in Chapter 3.

In addition to incorporating protective elements into the main security issued, companies can also enhance the potential return to the investor by issuing warrants along with the main security. In this fashion, the investor also holds securities having the right, but not the obligation, to exercise and exchange for common stock at such time as would be profitable to the investor. Through the use of warrants, the investor's return is enhanced through potential upside appreciation, rather than downside protection. The aggregate value to the investor can be augmented by increasing the number of warrants or by lowering the exercise price.

However, there is one key caveat to keep in mind. If an investor demands overly onerous terms, the cost to the company to acquire the

Downside protections to the investor
can come in many forms.

necessary cash could, in the end, result in significant dilution to the existing shareholders, and could even lead to insolvency. The company, in conjunction with its advisors, should perform cost-benefits analysis to assess the impact of any potential financing on the company.

We have now spelled out at a high level the two basic frameworks that characterize PIPE transactions. This information, however, can only remain theoretical without a means of translating and applying it to your company's financial needs. In that spirit, let us now integrate what we have covered so far with a specific model that you can use to determine which framework might be currently available to your company as you consider moving forward with a PIPE. We call it the FATE Model™.

Using the FATE Model™

This distinction between fundamental and technical deals really comes to life when you analyze the business characteristics of your company, the market characteristics of your stock, and how the interplay of those two factors will influence the kind of framework most suitable for your company and likely to be attractive to investors, and the steps you might be able to take to reposition the company if you are not currently satisfied with the financing options available to you

When working with clients at the beginning of our analysis, we like to walk them through our FATE Model™ as a means of determining what kind of framework they might expect for their PIPE (Figure 4). The acronym stands for Fundamental And Technical Evaluation.

The company, in conjunction with its advisors,
should perform cost-benefits analysis
to assess the impact of any potential
financing on the company.

Figure 4: The FATE Model™

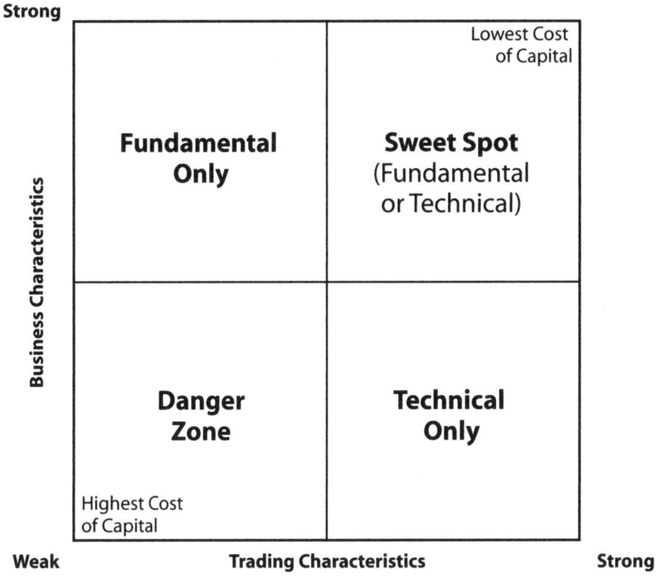

As the model shows, the kind of PIPE deal you can expect will be based on the interplay of both the strengths and weaknesses of your company's business characteristics (the vertical axis on the model) and those of the market characteristics of your stock (the horizontal axis). As you move from left to right and up the scale on the model, the cost of capital to your company *decreases* correspondingly.

In using this model to determine the appropriate PIPE framework for your company, you need to:

- Locate where your company currently falls on the grid (we suggest that you also think about where your competitors fit on the model and how that might explain the kinds of financing they have been doing.)

- Identify the kind of investors associated with each quadrant and how you want to deal with them.

- Assess what you can do to change your position if you aren't satisfied with where you presently fall on the grid and the options available to you.

Let's briefly review each quadrant in the model to see how you can use it as a tool. We'll approach the model clockwise.

Fundamental Only	Sweet Spot (Fundamental or Technical)
Danger Zone	Technical Only

In the upper-left quadrant, you are generally dealing from a position of strength as your company's business characteristics are attractive. However, an overall weakness in the trading market for your stock may limit the number of investors willing to get involved due to liquidity constraints associated with a relatively inactive trading market.

Fundamental Only	Sweet Spot (Fundamental or Technical)
Danger Zone	Technical Only

We call the upper right quadrant the Sweet Spot. This is where everybody would like to be. You have a great story and the trading market is active. Thus you can structure your deal *either* as a fundamental or technical one, depending on what you want to do and when you want to do it, how you want to allocate risk, and the type of investor you wish to attract. The Sweet Spot provides maximum flexibility to the company.

Fundamental Only	Sweet Spot (Fundamental or Technical)
Danger Zone	Technical Only

In the lower right quadrant, you need to confront the fact that your company's story leaves something to be desired. As such, there's not much likelihood that investors will be interested in a fundamental deal. However, this is somewhat compensated for by a strong trading market. Thus opportunities exist for technical deals, but you need to carefully consider the attractions and risks of any given structure. (We'll be covering exactly how to do that in more detail in the following chapters.) In this quadrant, it's critical to know the dangers that your company may face before moving forward with a transaction. This is especially true as you move toward the lower-left quadrant.

Fundamental Only	Sweet Spot (Fundamental or Technical)
Danger Zone	Technical Only

We call the lower left quadrant the Danger Zone (in our more pessimistic moods, we are tempted to call it the Dead Zone instead). In either case it's not an attractive place to be. Your company's story is weak and so is the trading market, so this is the territory where your options are greatly limited and where the possibilities of toxic PIPEs and death spirals become a grim reality. The cost of capital is at its highest and the number of safeguards that must be built into the deal to attract investors places the majority of risk squarely on the company—not a very attractive situation. The risk here is that the oppressive nature of the financing instrument will send the company's stock into a tailspin and push the company off the grid entirely. What does this mean? The terms of the PIPE create enormous pressure on the stock price. As the stock price declines, additional pressure is created that drives the stock price down even further. Ultimately, the stock price can fall so low that the company's stock is delisted and no longer trades publicly, making it all the more difficult to raise the additional capital needed to survive.

In addition to understanding where your company falls on the chart, it's necessary to think about what kinds of investors you're likely to deal with as a result. In effect you need to ask, "Who are the investors and how do they intend to create a return on their investment?" The answers to these questions reveal that distinctly different types of investors like to play at different parts of the grid.

Clearly investors at the upper left quadrant (fundamental only) are more likely to have interests aligned with those of the company and to be in it for the long haul. They are making their buying decision principally on the financial strength of the company. The weak trading market for the company's stock precludes participation by the short-term investor looking for a quick "flip," as the liquidity on the investment is too low. Their expectation is that the stock price will rise over time as the company's fortune rises.

Conversely, investors at the lower right quadrant (technical only) have far less interest in the fundamentals of the company itself. In fact, they may be totally indifferent! Their concern is entirely focused on liquidity and other market characteristics of the company's stock. Therefore, this group of investors places emphasis on how the deal is structured to ensure a positive return on their investment regardless of what happens to the company in the long-term.

Just as clearly, this tendency becomes even further pronounced as a given company slides from this quadrant toward the left and into the Danger Zone. In that quadrant, one may be faced with a species of predatory investor who may be looking to take advantage of the company's compromised position to extract egregious investment terms that benefit no one but the investor.

Having said all this, we wish also to make the point that the FATE Model™ is a simplification of a complex reality—indeed, its usefulness lies in its very simplicity. It is a decision-making tool designed to capture in a snapshot not only where you are today, but also where you might want to go in the future. In explaining the model at a high level, it is useful to describe the company as simply being positioned in one of the four quadrants, whereas in reality the company's position can be anywhere on the grid, and its relative position within a quadrant is an important factor as well.

The role of the CEO is to consider the company's present positioning on the grid and determine whether actions can or should be taken to shift the company from one quadrant into other. Clearly, different changes require a varying amount of lead time for effective implementation. Some changes can be effected in the short term; others take far longer. This brings to mind the example of one our clients who was told that his company could only do a technical deal. Our assessment of the situation was that this recommendation was based on a false and outdated perception of the company's story, both by the investment bank giving the advice and by the larger investment community. Rather than simply facing the inevitability of doing a technical deal, the client also had the option of making a concerted effort to communicate his company's new story. In this case, a strong roadshow presentation coupled with a fundamental deal was effective. By taking minimal action, the company was able to shift itself from the lower right quadrant of the model (technical deals only) up into the Sweet Spot (both technical and fundamental deals).

In summary, you can use the FATE Model™ to identify the financing framework realistically available to you and your company. Once you have done so, you are in a position to take appropriate action to get the deal you want, or at least to negotiate the best deal possible given your unique circumstances. Often times the key to better deal terms for the company is clear, effective communication of the company's story to the investor community and understanding the subtle nuances of the proposed deal structure. Helping you do just that is the focus of our next chapter.

CHAPTER 3

BASIC DEAL STRUCTURES

A t this point you have analyzed your company's overall story and made an initial determination regarding your company's position on the FATE Model™. Based on this analysis, you can begin working with your advisor to decide whether to do a technical deal or a fundamental deal—ideally, you will have both options. How do these frameworks affect how a PIPE is put together in the real world? The next step involves deciding what kind of deal structure you wish to create for your PIPE within the given framework. By *deal structure*, we mean the kinds of securities (with attendant features) that you will offer to prospective investors.

Not surprisingly, PIPE deal structures can take many forms and may include the use of one or more types of securities in combination. In the simplest terms, a security is a special form of legal instrument sold to an investor that represents some form of claim against the assets of the company. There are a number of securities that fall within this simple definition, including common stock, warrants, preferred stock, convertible preferred stock, and convertible debt. The PIPE investor typically purchases common stock or another security that can be converted into common stock, which is subsequently registered and traded on the public market. The ability to trade as registered common stock is the investor's means of eventually "exiting" the transaction, hopefully capturing a gain in the process. The heart of any given PIPE deal thus involves such questions as how the investor will be compensated for periods of illiquidity, how the security will be priced, and what forms of protection will be offered to balance the degree of risk being assumed by both investor and issuer.

Given this, the two most common types of securities used to create this structure and drive PIPE transactions are:

- **Common stock.** This type of deal structure typically involves selling an unregistered block of the company's common stock to a private investor at a negotiated discount to the current market price. The

The driving force of a PIPE structure is how risk is allocated between the company and the investors.

shares are generally sold with registration rights requiring the issuer to register the shares for resale by the investor in the public market. Terms are dependent upon the company's general condition, industry, trading patterns, volume, and current market environment. One variant of this form is a unit deal, generally composed of common stock and warrants.

- **Convertible securities.** In this type of deal structure, the company issues securities convertible into common stock, such as convertible debt (including debentures and notes) and convertible equity (preferred stock). The company registers the underlying common stock on behalf of the investor so that it can be traded by the investor at a future date. In this form of PIPE structure, certain protections are built in to shield the investor from the risks inherent in dealing with common stock alone. A deal structure based on convertible securities can therefore be very flexible and may be individually tailored to account for the amount of risk being assumed. (We will discuss those protections and features in more detail in Chapter 4.)

Securities can be used and combined in myriad ways within an overall fundamental or technical framework. A key point to keep in mind is that no two PIPEs are exactly alike: PIPEs allow for a tremendous amount of creativity and customization within their structure. *The driving force of a PIPE structure is how risk is allocated between the company and the investors.* To illustrate this, Figure 5 compares the basic characteristics of a fundamental PIPE deal with a technical PIPE deal.

Figure 5: Basic Characteristics of a
        Fundamental PIPE versus a Technical PIPE

Fundamental	Technical
• Typically structured as common stock deal	• Generally structured as convertible securities deal
• No additional protections offered for investors	• Layering on of levels of protection to make instrument more attractive
• Investors interested more in nature of company than structure of deal	• Investors interested more in structure of deal than nature of company
• Investors willing to accept risk to achieve maximum upside if company prospers	• Features offered that sweeten the deal and shift allocation of risk to company if things go badly
• Investors truly stakeholders in company	• Investors usually have no intention of holding the stock for extended period of time
• Investors "last in line" with other common shareholders if there is a liquidation of company	• Investors often have liquidation preference over common shareholders

The relationship between fundamental and technical deals can further be illustrated by considering the case of two investors in two separate PIPE transactions. In each case, the investor wants to invest $1 million into a company doing a PIPE offering. Investor A is driven by the business fundamentals of the company, while Investor B is interested in the market characteristics of the company's stock. (For purposes this chapter, we have assumed that fundamental deals will be common stock deals and that technical deals will be convertible deals to simplify the concepts. Bear in mind, however, that fundamental deals can be structured as fixed price convertibles and technical deals can be structured as common stock with resets—which is discussed more in Chapter 4—along with other downside protections for the investors.) The implications of this are sketched out in Figure 6.

In reality, most PIPE deals are not purely one thing or another: each has its unique structure based on various combinations of securities and features.

Figure 6: A Tale of Two Investors

	Investor A	Investor B
Initial investment	Buys 100,000 shares of common stock @ $10 per share (for an initial investment of $1 million)	Buys a $1 million convertible preferred security (CPS), with an initial conversion price of $10 per share (worth 100,000 shares)
Protective features	None	If the market price drops, the investor will be able to convert at the lower market price (if the market price rises, the investor can still convert at $10 per share)
Assumption of risk	Completely on the investor (in effect the company is "done" once it issues the stock and gets its money)	Shifted onto company (it may have to issue additional shares to make investor whole if the market price drops)
Scenario 1: The market price falls to $8 per share	The investor owns 100,000 shares worth $8 per share—representing a loss of $200,000	Investor can convert the CPS into common stock at $8 per share, so the $1 million convertible security is now worth 125,000 shares, which the investor can sell for $1 million and "exit" without losing any money
Scenario 2: The market price rises to $12 per share	The investor owns 100,000 shares worth $12 per share—representing a gain of $200,000	Investor can convert the CPS into common stock at $10 per share, so the $1 million convertible security is still worth 100,000 shares, which the investor can sell for $1.2 million and "exit" by making the same $200,000 gain as the common stock investor without having assumed any of the risk

Let's now examine in more detail how each of these can structured. (We will then examine a hybrid form of deal structure, the structured equity line.)

Common Stock

In examining common stock deals, we'll focus on the following:

- Deals where common stock is sold at a premium to market

- Deals where common stock is sold at a discount

Common Stock at a Premium to Market

In the case of a strong company or story, while investors might like features that provide downside protection, they may not be in a position to demand them and must purchase common stock if they want to invest in a company (or perhaps common stock with some warrants added). In some cases, investors may even be willing to invest at a *premium*—they realize that purchasing a large block of stock on the open market would likely raise the purchase price, and therefore they would be better off buying a block of stock directly from the company at a premium.

Whether large blocks of stock are sold at a premium or discount often depends significantly on the perspective of who is driving the transaction: the buyer or the seller. An issuer who wants to sell a large block of stock and then finds investors to buy the block may need to sell at a discount. But when an investor wants to purchase a block from the company and is driving the transaction, it may have to pay a premium to do so. In other words, at any given moment, the price of the securities is driven by the basic economic concept of supply versus demand. When demand exceeds supply, the price increases, and when supply exceeds demand, the price decreases.

Common stock deals effected at a premium to market can also be private investments by strategic partners where the equity investment is part of a larger collaboration or strategic relationship where the investor is receiving other business benefits as part of the deal (for example, access to proprietary technology or established distribution). In such cases, the investor is seeking a long-term relationship with the company and often the company is using the proceeds for the investment to fund the collaborative efforts. Such investors usually are not concerned with short-term liquidity for their investment. The strategic investment also sends a signal to the market that the partner is committed to the relationship and believes in the future potential of the company.

Discounted Common Stock

Discounted common stock (or discounted common stock with warrants) is the favored investment vehicle for fundamental deals. The price is set at a discount to some proxy for the current market price.[1] The discount is established through negotiations between the company and the investors. Just prior to signing the purchase agreement, the actual price is established based upon an agreed-upon pricing formula (for example, a 10 percent discount from the five-day trailing average closing stock price). The investor receives these discounts or warrants not because the story is weak, but rather to compensate for the additional risk of holding an unregistered, restricted security that is untradable—and therefore illiquid—for some period of time; thus the longer the period, the higher the associated discount.

Convertible Securities

In our focus on convertible securities, we'll look at:

- The issue of convertible debt versus convertible preferred stock

- Typical conversion features

Convertible Debt or Preferred Stock

Technical deals often take the form of convertible securities, either convertible debt or convertible preferred stock, because of the structural flexibility provided by these securities. These two securities can be very

---

[1] Many follow-on public offerings are priced at the market, therefore no discount, but the stock price typically moves downward on the basis of anticipated dilution following the filing of the offering, so that the effective discount to market can be substantial.

Conversion caps and pricing floors can be incorporated into a PIPE structure to limit the amount of potential dilution to a known maximum amount.

Similar in terms of their conversion features, but debt has a higher priority on liquidation so convertible debt is a safer bet for the investor (it carries a fixed obligation of repayment at maturity, combined with the option to convert to equity) and can be cheaper for the issuing company. Since the conversion option is valuable to the holder, the interest rate on the convertible debt is lower than a similar straight debt security. In addition, if the instrument is never converted, the company avoids additional equity dilution. However, unlike common stock, convertible debt requires the company to pay principal and interest, which are additional burdens on the issuer.

A convertible preferred stock issue, with or without a fixed dividend, is often negotiated to provide a balance of upside potential and priority of claim to the investor, while allowing the company to issue equity, not debt. Bear in mind, however, that from an accounting perspective, this type of security is often treated as a mezzanine instrument rather than pure equity.

A convertible security with a *fixed* conversion rate will convert at that rate for the life of the security, regardless of changes in the underlying stock price. A convertible with a *floating* or *adjustable* rate (used for riskier transactions) will convert at different rates over the life of the security, in accordance with a conversion price formula agreed to at the closing of the PIPE transaction (details regarding conversion features are contained in the next chapter).

The most significant issue with convertibles is the amount of potential *dilution* to current equity holders resulting from the conversion of the convertible debt or convertible preferred stock into common stock. This is especially a concern where the price of the underlying stock has declined substantially and the conversion price formula is tied to this stock price. The conversion price will drop as the stock price decreases, thereby increasing the number of shares issued upon conversion and further diluting the existing stockholders. While this relationship has given rise to the names "toxic" and "death spiral," dilution (as discussed earlier) can be anticipated and controlled through such mechanisms as conversion caps and pricing floors. These structures limit the amount of dilution to a

Equity lines can be a highly effective capital-raising tool for a company where the liquidity of its stock is sufficient to support the introduction of additional shares into the market.

known maximum amount (again, full details can be found in the following chapter).

A convertible security with a reset price mechanism is essentially a hybrid between a fixed convertible and an adjustable convertible. As with an adjustable pricing formula, a reset pricing formula allows the conversion price to change during the life of the security. However, unlike an adjustable, the conversion price only adjusts at pre-set intervals or upon the occurrence of agreed-upon events (for example, the conversion price adjusts to the market price on the one-year anniversary of the instrument, if the market price is lower than the initial conversion price). Any other movements in the stock price in the interim do not cause the conversion price to adjust.

Convertibles are often *callable* or *redeemable*—in other words, the issuer may redeem the security during a stated period at a previously negotiated price. The redemption price is usually the issue price plus any accrued, unpaid interest or dividends plus a call premium. Generally, when the conversion value exceeds the call price, the issuers can—and often do—force conversion by giving notice of redemption to the investors.

Conversion Price Mechanism Summary

In summary, a convertible debenture or convertible preferred stock generally has one of three conversion price mechanisms:

- **Fixed-price convertibles.** These are securities that have a single fixed conversion price, generally determined on the closing date or some agreed-upon future date, and are convertible at that price for the entire term of the security.

- **Variable or floating-price convertibles.** Floating-price and variable-price securities have an adjustable conversion price generally based on the future market price of the common stock at the time of conversion.

- **Reset convertibles.** Resets are securities that are a hybrid between a fixed-price convertible and a variable or floating-price convertible where the conversion price is reset at agreed-upon intervals.

An equity line only makes sense
if there is sufficient trading volume
in the company's common stock.

Structured Equity Lines: A Hybrid PIPE Structure

Until now, we have focused on PIPEs with fundamental and technical deal structures. There is also an interesting hybrid security, a structured equity line, which is a combination of a PIPE and a public offering. In this discussion we shall focus on:

- Basic definitions and examples

- Advantages and disadvantages

- Guidelines for proper use

- Typical misconceptions

Basic Definitions and Examples

With a structured equity line, the investor commits to purchase up to a predetermined dollar amount or number of shares of the company's common stock over a certain period, with the timing of stock sales at the option of the issuer. It is similar to a bank line of credit, in that cash is available to the company on an as-needed basis, but the company "repays" the investor with stock rather than cash. The company has the right, but not the obligation, to periodically draw down on the equity line (a "put") and sell shares to the investor when it is favorable for the company to do so. Upon a drawdown, the shares are then sold to the investor at a previously negotiated discount to the market price of the shares at the time of the put. The investor sells the shares into the marketplace and captures the spread between the price paid to the company and the proceeds received from the sale of the shares into the market.

Equity lines can be a highly effective capital-raising tool for a company where the liquidity of its stock is sufficient to support the introduction of additional shares into the market. For such a company, introducing a limited number of additional shares of stock into the market should not materially disrupt the market trading price of the stock. As a general rule of thumb, the market can absorb approximately 10 to 15 percent of the company's daily trading volume. The main trading characteristics of the company (share price, market capitalization, and daily trading volume of its common stock) must be sufficient to bear the new securities periodically coming out on the market.

The company should understand that equity line investors are generally not long-term investors—equity lines are basically an arbitrage play for the investor. The key benefit is that the company is able to raise money on an as-needed basis at a nominal discount to the current market price. Remember, *an equity line only makes sense if there is sufficient trading volume in the company's common stock.*

As an example of an equity line, consider the following case study. Investor Save-em Fund, LLC commits to purchase $10 million of common stock in the company Bleeding Cash, Inc. during a period of two years. Bleeding Cash will have the right (no more frequently than every 30 days) to put, or sell (a "drawdown"), up to $1 million of common stock to Save-em Fund (a draw) upon 15 trading days' notice. The price of the common stock purchased by investor Save-em is 95 percent of the average daily price for a specified number of days preceding the draw. With each draw notice, Bleeding Cash will specify the minimum price at which it is willing to sell shares. No shares will be sold below this price. Investor Save-em may choose to sell the shares being put to it and may begin to do so upon notice of the drawdown. If the equity line is structured properly, Save-em will be contractually limited to selling only those shares that it is about to receive in the drawdown and the amount will be nominal compared to daily trading volume so the shares will be quickly and quietly absorbed into the marketplace.

Equity Line Advantages Over Public Offerings

When structured properly, the equity line has numerous advantages over public financings, including spot secondaries:

• **Equity lines provide standby capital similar to a traditional line of credit.** Like a debt facility, there is a maximum total commitment by the investor (lender) and periodic availability of capital under the line. Unlike a credit line, however, the company will never be required to repay the investor since it is issuing equity in exchange for cash.

- **The company has absolute discretion over the timing, amount, and price of the equity it will sell.** The company can set a floor price, which is the minimum price at which it will sell its shares. The company does not sell any shares to the investor below the floor price. If the market price falls below the floor price during a drawdown, then no additional shares are sold.

- **The company can take advantage of volatile spikes in its stock price.** The company can obtain equity infusions under the equity line from time to time, and the price at which the company sells its equity therefore floats with the then-prevailing market prices (less a nominal discount). Because the investor always purchases shares at the negotiated discount to the market price, it doesn't matter whether the stock is trading at a high or at a low relative to historic levels.

- **Common stock is sold at a priced based upon prevailing market prices.** The discount is typically lower than the effective price discount after a follow-on public offering is filed and the stock falls in anticipation of dilution related to the share issuance.

- **Pricing of the equity line structure is straightforward.** There are no complicated conversion formulas, default provisions, or risks of unanticipated dilution.

An equity line investor is considered to be an underwriter under the securities laws and may elect to sell or hold the shares. If they sell, a properly structured equity line will allow them to only sell up to the number of shares that will be issued to them in the draw down.

Equity Lines Require the Right Conditions

An equity line can be a powerful, highly effective capital-raising tool under the right conditions. Under the wrong circumstances, an equity line can create overhang that limits upside and entices short-selling and dilution. The right conditions include limiting the overall size of the equity line related to market capitalization of the company, and limiting the amount the company can draw down and sell to the investor at any one time. Generally, the drawdown amount is limited to 10 to 15 percent

When properly structured, an equity line of credit
can provide companies with the flexibility to
access cash they need when they need it,
at a nominal discount to the market price.

of the company's daily trading volume. A greater amount tends to create excess supply and corresponding downward pressure on the company's stock price. An equity line works very well when used by a company as an opportunistic mechanism to supplement working capital.

Another potential pitfall that can be protected against is predictability of draw-downs. If the market can accurately anticipate the size and timing of company drawdowns, then other parties not involved in the transaction may attempt to profit by shorting the company's stock. Therefore, it is important that the company's behavior be somewhat unpredictable in order to protect its stock price during drawdown periods.

Equity Lines—Another Bum Rap

When properly structured with the features outlined here and in the next chapter, an equity line can provide companies with the flexibility to access the cash they need when they need it, at a nominal discount to the market price.

It should be noted that equity lines have their skeptics, and certain investors have been very vocal in this area. Their concerns are twofold. First, they ask, "Why would an investor who believes a company's stock will rise *not* try to buy as much of the stock as possible upfront?" The reality is that equity lines are not typically purchased by long-term equity investors, but rather are an arbitrage vehicle where the investor merely facilitates the placement of shares into the market. Second, skeptics are concerned that the providers of equity lines have an incentive to short the stock in the time between a company's saying it wants to sell some stock and the purchase is actually made. A properly structured equity line agreement prohibits this type of shorting activity. Finally, they fear that shares purchased are usually sold quickly on the open market, thereby depressing stock prices. If equity lines are properly structured, the volume of shares sold on any given drawdown is so small relative to the average daily trading volume that the shares are absorbed without materially depressing the stock price.

While a PIPE can provide a company with the lifeblood of business—cash—company management must then execute their business model successfully for the company to prosper, regardless of the financing vehicle chosen.

Two Key Conclusions

Let's conclude this chapter with two things to consider while discussing any PIPE structure: PIPEs are not a panacea and structures are not inherently evil.

Conclusion 1: PIPEs Are Not a Panacea

PIPE structures can use any legally available form of security to allocate the risk of the transaction onto the appropriate party. An expert advisor will assist the company by structuring the PIPE transaction and leading the negotiations to balance the needs of both the company and the investor. All this being said, it remains the fact that good management and a good story or fundamentals are always needed for a company to thrive and prosper. A troubled company with poor management and an unsustainable business model is a bad investment, period. PIPEs have been indiscriminately blamed for the demise of a number of weak companies using them. This logic assumes causation where it does not necessarily exist. PIPEs are not a panacea for a fundamentally flawed company. While a PIPE can provide a company with the lifeblood of business—cash—company management must then execute their business model successfully for the company to prosper, regardless of the financing vehicle chosen.

Conclusion 2: Structures Are Not Inherently Evil

In working with clients, we sometimes encounter executives who have heard that certain financing structures are fundamentally bad for a company and therefore are beyond consideration. We'll hear a CEO say, "I'm not doing any of those preferred convertible deals. They're toxic." Although we respect these concerns, we try to make the point that a given structure, in and of itself, is not necessarily evil. You shouldn't be afraid to do a convertible deal because of rumors of bad deals. Properly structured, there are a number of securities that can offer both a tremendous degree of flexibility and protection for both parties while ensuring the company gets the money it needs now.

In short, if the deal is structured properly with the right features to protect the company, and if one is dealing with an investor who isn't simply a predator looking to profit by driving the company's stock price down, a convertible deal can be an excellent decision. Much of this will depend upon how the conversion price is set. Is it fixed? Is it floating? Does it reset? As an example, consider the following scenario. A company says to a potential PIPE investor, "Although we can't guarantee it to the market, we're very confident that in the next twelve months we're going to announce a major new pharmaceutical partner." Thus the deal could be structured so that if the company does announce the partnership within the next year, the stock price won't reset. However if deal doesn't happen then the conversion price may be reset to a certain figure; for example, the trailing average price over the previous twenty days or some such feature. As such, the company gets the money it needs now, at a better conversion price for the company, while sharing the risk with the investor who is afforded protection if the company can't actually deliver on its promise. If the company really believes in itself, this structure provides a means to balance risk and reward for both parties, and hardly seems to be an unfair trade-off or burden for the company or the investor.

Keeping this final maxim in mind, we see the absolute necessity of working with your advisor to carefully examine the features of any technical deal structure before signing off on the deal. Arming you with the information to do just that is the focus of our next chapter.

CHAPTER 4

LOOKING AT PIPE FEATURES

A t this stage we are moving deeper into the heart of creating a PIPE. We have already considered how to assess whether you should pursue a fundamental or technical deal, and we've also started thinking about the different securities available to us for creating a deal structure. As we've discussed, common stock or fixed-rate convertible securities are typically the investment vehicles of choice in fundamental deals. Fundamental investors invest based on the strength of the company's business prospects and are not as concerned with the trading characteristics of the company's stock. Conversely, securities that are priced in the future at a discount to the market price, such as a variable rate convertible security, represent a typical structure to support an investment made by a technical investor. Technical investors invest based on the trading characteristics of the company and are not as concerned with the underlying strength of the company's business prospects. They are not as confident that they will generate an acceptable return on the basis of business fundamentals alone, so they require certain protective mechanisms to enhance their potential return.

We will now move into a discussion of what we call the underlying *features* of the deal. We define features as the specific characteristics of the security or deal structure that define the rights and obligations of the investors and the company. These characteristics include the pricing mechanism, timing considerations, deal covenants, and other restrictive provisions. For fundamental deals, the defining features are relatively straightforward and will be largely a matter of determining the price per share based on the appropriate valuation for the company. As discussed earlier, it is the relative simplicity of common stock deals that makes them attractive to both the company and the investors. However, this simplicity is lost when a deal is structured as a technical investment. The complexity of the features and provisions incorporated in a technically structured deal can be daunting and difficult for CEOs to decipher, regardless of their financing experience. Most investors see the inclusion of the various features as part of a continuum. They will be looking to achieve a particular return and will view the deal features as part of a trade-off in which they may be willing to accept a particular feature that the company wants to have (or wants to exclude) in exchange for something the investor wants. It is important that the CEO fully understand the various features and their potential impact in order to negotiate effectively—features can be built into (or omitted from) a PIPE that will create an investment vehicle that:

- Shifts the burden of risk toward the investors—in some cases, the company will ask for an unreasonable valuation for the company or for features that are far too restrictive, such that an investment is not attractive for even the most fundamental investors

- Strikes an equitable balance in its distribution of risk between the issuing company and its investors

- Allocates more risk towards the company—in some cases, the vehicle may provide the company with quick cash, but cause significant dilution in the long term

- Places the entire risk on the company—this is defined as the reviled toxic or death spiral financing, where the investor will make as much or more money when the stock goes down than when the stock goes up

The objective in negotiating features is to find the point at which the distribution of risk is fair to both the company and investor, taking into account the company's specific situation and the realities of the current market. Figure 7 illustrates this concept:

Figure 7: A CEO's Sense of Balance

Investor Technical Deal		Company Fundamental Deal
←———————	"Balance Point"	———————→
• Riskier		• Safer
• Many unknowns		• Defined and clear
• Opportunity higher for both parties		• Paying for/limited by deal's "sense of simplicity"
• Greater likelihood of being deceptive with so many options and features in play		• Potentially deceptive beneath simplicity

In this chapter, we will concentrate on the flexibility inherent in PIPE deals that provide the means to shift risk between the investor and the company. We will begin our discussion with convertible securities, the most common instrument used in structuring technical deals. We will then discuss common stock deals and warrants. We will start our examination of convertible securities with some general guidelines on pricing.

Convertible Securities: General Pricing Guidelines

How do we define a convertible security? In simple terms, a convertible security is either debt or preferred stock with an embedded call option to buy the common stock of the issuer. Therefore, when pricing a convertible security, one must consider two aspects of value in general: first, the security's coupon or dividend rate, and second, the value of the embedded call option.

Pricing the coupon or dividend rate. Due to the extra value of the call, the coupon rate of a convertible will be lower than a similar non-convertible security for the same company. While there are a number of valuation models designed to determine the appropriate interest rate or dividend rate, the pricing of the interest rate or dividend rate on straight debt and preferred stock, respectively, is actually set by the market based on a number of factors, including supply and demand, comparisons to other recently priced deals, deals that are trading, and the current interest rate environment. In order to achieve the lowest possible dividend or interest rate, the company and its advisors must highlight the unique strengths of the company to demonstrate the ability of the company to repay its obligations under the note.

Conversion price. The conversion price is the price per share at which a convertible security can be converted into common shares. By investing in a convertible security, an investor is afforded upside if the underlying equity appreciates in value. In addition, companies like to be able to sell stock today at a premium to the market. How does this work? The investor receives interest or dividend on the convertible debt or convertible preferred, however, the dividend or interest rate is lower than the company would pay if the security was not convertible. The higher the premium

Conversion value = # of shares receivable upon
conversion at conversion ratio
x
market price of the stock

Value of convertible debt = straight value + value
of the call option on the underlying common stock

on the conversion price, the more the convertible security looks like a nonconvertible security and the interest or dividend rate approaches that of a nonconvertible security.

Pricing the embedded call option. Since a convertible security grants the holder a call option, one component of the total value of the convertible is the fair market value of the embedded call. The theoretical value of a call option can be calculated using one of a number of theoretical option pricing models (such as the Black-Scholes formula or the binomial method) One of the most critical variables in the Black-Scholes formula is the expected price volatility of the underlying common stock. The greater the expected volatility, the greater the call value. It is beyond the scope of this text to explain exactly how the Black-Scholes formula works, however, if you are interested in learning more about this topic, there are many corporate finance texts available that provide detailed explanations regarding the Black-Scholes formula.

The Black-Scholes formula makes certain simplifying assumptions, including a perfectly liquid trading market. An instrument that is not public and does not trade at all requires a significant discount for a lack of marketability to determine its fair value. (Remember, it is the underlying common stock that will be registered, traded, and provide liquidity, not the convertible instrument issued in the PIPE.) When running Black-Scholes for an illiquid investment, you must incorporate a significant discount for lack of marketability.

Keeping these guidelines in mind, let's now drill down even further into the features that can potentially come into play for any deal structure based on convertible securities.

Convertible Securities Features

When structuring a convertible security the following questions will be paramount to your investors:

- How will the securities be converted into common stock to provide liquidity? This involves such issues as defining the conversion price,

When running Black-Scholes for an illiquid investment, you must incorporate a significant discount for lack of marketability.

setting limits (both high and low) to that price, and building in any antidilution protective features.

- Will dividends or interest be paid? If so, how? Cash or stock? And what formula will be used for evaluating and pricing stock?

- Will there be a redemption feature built into the security? If so, how will it be defined? How will it be invoked? And by whom?

- Will there be any additional defining conditions or restrictions on how this conversion can take place? Who will they benefit and protect?

In short, there are many questions and issues to be defined and resolved between the company and the investors. In Figure 8, we have summarized what we consider to be the most critical variables in play when you consider doing a convertible security deal. We will then examine each of these feature sets in more detail as we move through the chapter. Keep in mind that we will address common stock and warrants as separate forms of securities later in this chapter.

Figure 8: Features of a Convertible Security Deal Structure

Conversion Price			Dividends	Redemption	Covenants/ Restrictions
Price Formulas	Floors/ Ceilings	Price Protection (Anti-Dilution)	Cash, stock, or PIK	Cash, stock, or PIK	

– Fixed
– Floating
– Reset
	– Hard
	– Soft
	– Green
		– Ratchet
		  * Full
		  * Partial
		– Time to 1st conversion
		– Monthly conversion limit
			– What formula will be used for pricing stock for PIK (payment-in-kind)—Market Value, trailing average, and so on?	– Forced Conversion
				– Who has the right to call or put?
				(Call = right to buy
				Put = right to sell)
					– Short-selling
					– Lock-Up Periods
					– Cap on shares issuable
					– Limitations on subsequent financings

At first glance, this can seem like a formidable list to try and keep in mind while doing any PIPE. We do not mean to minimize the complexities involved. An inherent respect for all of the features in play for a given PIPE is critical to truly understanding the potential risks and maximizing protection to your company. The complexity involved accentuates the

Reset events
can be linked to virtually anything.

need for a trusted financial advisor to help you negotiate your way through these issues. Above all, our goal here is to arm you with enough information that you can understand the fundamentals and be able to participate comfortably in any discussion as an informed participant. With that in mind, let's walk through each of these feature sets.

Conversion Price Formulas

Many convertible security features are *optional* items in any given PIPE deal, but defining the conversion price is a *mandatory* element that lies at the heart of any such transaction. Therefore, we plan to focus on that area in some detail. In our discussion, we will cover:

- What are the basic definitions for each conversion formula?

- How do resets work?

- What are the dangers inherent in dealing with "floating-rate" convertibles?

Basic Definitions

A convertible debenture or convertible preferred stock generally has one of three basic types of conversion formulas:

- **Fixed-price convertibles.** These securities have a single fixed conversion price, generally determined on the closing date, and are convertible at that price for the entire term of the security. These are appropriate for fundamental deals where the upside potential from conversion is a sufficient sweetener to the investor and the investor does not need further downside protection in order to be convinced to participate in the transaction.

- **Variable or floating-price convertibles.** These securities have a variable or freely floating conversion price that is typically a discount to the future market price of the underlying common stock at the time of conversion. Floating-price convertibles give the investor downside protection on the amount they invested, in that if there is a decline in the market price of the underlying common stock, there is a corresponding reduction in the conversion price and the investor will receive additional shares upon conversion equal to the difference.

- **Reset convertibles.** These securities are a hybrid between a fixed-price convertible and a variable or floating-price convertible where the conversion price is reset at previously agreed upon intervals or upon previously agreed upon events. The key difference between reset and variable pricing mechanisms is that with a reset, the price only changes at certain points in time, where as with variable pricing, the conversion price moves continuously with the market. To help you visualize the differences, see Figure 9.

Figure 9: Comparing Variable, Fixed, and Resets

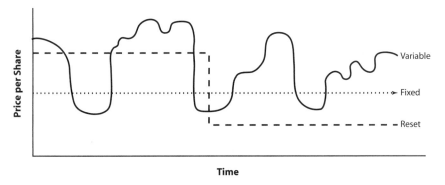

How Do Resets Work?

Given their hybrid status, there can be some uncertainty about how resets actually work. First, it is critical to keep in mind that reset events are negotiable and can be linked to virtually anything. Resets give investors another layer of protection, and investors may ask for more reset events if they feel that the company's story is lacking or weak. Generally, the higher the quality of the company, the *fewer* the resets.

Typically, resets are based on the following events:

- **Stock price performance.** If the stock price declines by more than an agreed-upon percentage below the current conversion price for five continuous trading days then the conversion price will reset by a predetermined formula. Any declines less than the agreed-upon percentage will not trigger the reset.

- **Time intervals.** The conversion price may be reset monthly, quarterly, semi-annually, or annually at a formula based on prevailing market prices. In this case, nothing triggers the reset other than the passage of time.

- **Events or milestones:** If certain milestones or events are achieved within an agreed-upon timeframe, no reset occurs. If the milestone or event does not occur within the agreed-upon timeframe, then the conversion price is reset at that time in accordance with a formula based on prevailing market prices. We believe that milestone-based resets represent the best of both worlds for the company and investor. After all, the company is making certain statements and representations to the investor to make the company attractive. It is only fair that the company stands behind its own promises and shift some of the risk to itself in taking responsibility for its own story. In addition, unlike the variable pricing formula, the milestone-based reset approach eliminates the impact of unpredictable market volatility. Milestone or event-based reset formulas can be based on events within the company's control.

What Are the Dangers of Floating Prices?

Floating or variable conversion pricing can trigger a cascade effect where, as the investor sells, the market price and the related conversion price drops and the more the investor sells the more the conversion price drops. When conversion is uncontrolled—that is, without a floor— a death spiral or toxic deal can be the result. Therefore, *it is critical to use a floor when issuing a variable or floating-rate convertible.* Let's now continue with this subject by discussing how floors and ceilings are important features of a variable-rate convertible securities deal.

Floors and Ceilings

Simply put, when a variable rate convertible deal has no floor then dilution has no limit. Therefore, negotiating a proper floor in a convertible deal is one of the most important facets of a convertible PIPE transaction for an issuer.

Milestone or event-based reset formulas
can be based on events
within the company's control.

Of course, our goal here is not to dissuade you from considering convertible deals. As we stressed earlier, *convertible deals need not be toxic and need not turn into a death spiral.* An issuer must be knowledgeable of, and insist upon having, certain beneficial provisions built into the transaction to protect the company and its shareholders. Dilution can be controlled. Issuers can set floors on how low the convertible exercise price can decline. In addition, *issuers should always avoid deals where the investor makes more money if the stock price goes down than if it appreciates.*

There are three types of floor provisions a company should consider in order to prevent excessive dilution:

- **Hard floors.** A *hard price floor* prohibits any conversions from occurring at a price less than the floor price at any time. Alternatively, *a hard share floor* can limit the amount of shares that are issuable upon conversion, regardless of price, so that the conversion price can float with the market price, but the number of common shares that can be issued upon conversion is limited. Hard floors therefore provide an absolute maximum potential dilution that can occur from the PIPE transaction. A hard floor is the best and most stringent protection to an issuer issuing a convertible.

- **Soft Floors.** A *soft floor* allows deal terms to change if the company's stock price decreases or falls below a predetermined price. The company and the investor agree at the closing what terms will change if a drop in stock price of a preset amount occurs. The same deal can have a hard floor and a soft floor, offering multiple layers of protections for different parties.

- **Green Floors.** A *green floor* enables the company to redeem (buy back for cash, often at the original issuance price) the security when the variable conversion price falls below a previously agreed-upon price (which could be significantly below the original conversion price). While investors will earn no upside on those additional shares they

It is critical to use a floor when issuing
a variable- or floating-price convertible.

have yet to convert, if the company's stock price has tanked they will generally be happy to have the opportunity to get their money back. Otherwise they could be left with a large number of virtually worthless shares with a low conversion price, but with presumably declining liquidity in the market for this stock there is the potential of a significant delay before they would be able to convert and liquidate their investment (if at all). One additional note about green floors: practically speaking, if the company's stock price has declined dramatically, there is a good chance that the company will not have enough cash on hand to redeem. At such juncture, the investor may be willing to take a significant discount from its original investment just to minimize its losses. Your advisor will be able to work with you in these situations if they arise.

Anti-Dilution Protection

If a company continues to grow, successive financing rounds are completed at increasingly higher valuations. But sometimes things don't go quite as planned and the company is forced to complete a "down" round where the valuation of the company is lower than the previous round. Any discussion of convertible securities will involve a negotiation regarding whether the investor is entitled to any antidilution protection if the company does a subsequent offering of securities at a lower valuation. The investor wants to be protected if the company should issue new stock at a lower price and dilute the value of the securities the investor currently holds. From the company's point of view, the potential for a decline in the company's valuation is an ordinary risk of investing. Whether the investor receives antidilution protection is a negotiated point, the outcome of which is determined by which party has more bargaining power. The following discussion covers some of the more common antidilution protection mechanisms.

Protecting the Investor: Full and Partial Ratchets

Ratchet provisions come in two basic forms: full and partial. They can apply for an agreed-upon period of time or the life of the investment.

When a convertible has no floor,
dilution has no limit.

Similar to a ratchet wrench, this price protection mechanism only goes in one direction, down. If the company raises additional financing at a price lower than the investors paid in the current round, the ratchet provision kicks in and the price paid by the investors adjusts accordingly. With a full ratchet, the conversion price adjusts to equal the price in the current round, regardless of the number of shares issued. You might think this is fairly oppressive, and you would be right. For that reason, the partial ratchet is more typically used. With a partial ratchet, the conversion price adjusts, but on a weighted average basis that takes into account the number of shares outstanding prior to the down round and the number of shares currently being issued at the lower price. If the latest round is small, then the adjustment to the conversion price is minimal. As the size of the latest round increases, the adjustment under a partial ratchet approaches that of a full ratchet.

To make this more concrete, let's look at an example of how a full ratchet might work. Let's say that Company A raises $10 million from Investor B on the first of January at an initial conversion price of $5 per share. Six months pass and Company A decides it needs to raise another $8 million. This time, however, the conversion price being offered is only $3 a share. Under a "full ratchet," the conversion price for Investor B automatically ratchets down to $3 a share. As such, Investor B is being offered the benefit of the full drop in the conversion price as a form of protecting his initial (and proportional) investment.

However, let's say that the second fund raising effort was only for $200,000. In this case, a full ratchet would be oppressive. It doesn't seem equitable that the *entire* $10,000,000 investment of Investor B should be adjusted down to $3 per share. This example illustrates why a partial ratchet is more equitable. On a weighted average basis, the company would look at the money that has just been raised relative to the shares outstanding prior to the transaction. The company would then weight a proportional drop in the price for Investor B. In our example, since $200,000 is such a small amount relative to the number of shares outstanding, the new conversion price would only fall by a small amount,

Issuers should always avoid deals where
the investor makes more money if the stock price
goes down than if it appreciates.

perhaps to something like $4.80 (depending on the specific formula used) from the original $5 per share (as opposed to $3 under a full ratchet).

Protecting the Company: Defining Conversions

Ratchets are a form of price protection designed to protect the investor. However, anti-dilution measures are not a one-way street. We will now discuss two methods designed to protect the company.

- **Time to first conversion.** A company can negotiate that the investor refrain from converting its security into common stock for a certain period of time. This lock-up period gives the company time to utilize the money that it received from the PIPE financing and increase shareholder value before the investor puts any selling pressure on the stock. For example, the money may have been raised to file for FDA approval or to complete a pending acquisition. To the extent the company establishes positive momentum in the stock through such a development, demand for the stock should increase and offset any additional supply made available in the market through investor selling.

- **Monthly conversion limitation.** This limits the amount an investor can convert during any given monthly period. As mentioned earlier, in order to avoid excess pressure on the company's stock and a corresponding drop in stock price, company management needs to take measures such as this to limit the amount of stock being converted and sold at any given time. Monthly conversion limits should be set at a level that allows the investor to have liquidity on the investment, but at a reasonable pace that doesn't unnecessarily hurt the company's stock price.

Dividends and Interest Payments

As mentioned previously, defining the conversion price is the one mandatory feature in CPS deals. One optional feature, however, is whether or not the instrument will pay the investor a periodic distribution in the form of a dividend or interest payment. If so, these distributions can be designated as payable in cash or additional securities (payment-in-kind, or PIK) at either the company's or investor's option. This feature can also

Hard floors provide an absolute maximum
potential dilution that will and can occur in a PIPE.

be used to balance the parties' interests. For example, if a distribution is payable in cash or in kind at the company's option, then the company has the option to preserve cash by paying with stock. However, the trade-off is the additional dilution the company experiences by issuing stock in place of cash. Therefore, the attractiveness of the PIK feature depends on the price used to determine the number of shares paid to the investor. Not surprisingly, there are a number of formulas used for pricing the stock, including, but not limited to:

- Closing price on the day the distribution is paid

- Trailing average market-based price

- Formula-based pricing specified in the security (for example, a specified discount to market)

In effect the only limitations here are those of the imagination and what is acceptable to both parties.

A Note on Repayment of Debt

As with dividends, debt transactions can be structured so that at maturity, the obligations are repaid in securities (for example, registered common stock). Again, the company avoids the possibility of having to raise or use more cash, but sacrifices additional dilution. In order to be considered debt for favorable tax treatment, the instrument has to be repayable at maturity but it can be repaid in either *cash* or *securities*. If it is only payable in securities, it is treated as preferred stock and the interest payments will not be tax deductible.

Focusing on Redemption

Another optional feature of a convertible deal structure is redemption—the company's right to buy back the security under certain circumstances at a specified price. Depending upon how the deal is negotiated and structured, this redemption can take the form of either cash or securities. In the event the redemption involves the use of securities, the PIK features that we discussed earlier when we covered the dividend features of a convertible deal apply.

To be constituted as debt for favorable
tax treatment, the instrument has to be repayable
at maturity in either cash or securities.

Redemption provisions give the company flexibility in the event of changed circumstances. By notifying the investor of its intent to redeem following appreciation in the stock price, the company essentially forces the investor to convert some or all of its securities into common stock in order to capture the gain. Redemption rights are attractive to the company for a number of reasons. For example, a company may want to exercise such rights when its stock rises significantly, but the investor may still have an interest in holding the convertible security for its option value. In anticipation of another financing, the company can use the redemption provision to eliminate the overhang associated with the "in-the-money" convertible security. There are also circumstances where the investor might want to force the company to repurchase the security. These forced redemption rights can be broadly categorized as *calls and puts*, depending upon who has the right to force the redemption:

- If the company can redeem the security, then the company has a *call*, or the right to buy. The company is telling the investor, "You can't leave that convertible lying out there forever. If certain things happen, we have the right to buy it back from you."

- Conversely, the investor may also have the right to force the company to redeem, in other words, to buy back the security. This is known as a *put*, or the right to sell. The investor in this case is not looking to convert the stock and trade, but instead wants to recover its original investment amount by forcing the company to buy back the security.

Covenants and Restrictions

Various negotiated trading restrictions can place limitations on short selling, hedging, and selling activity by the investor. In this discussion of covenants and restrictions, we will pay particular attention to the following:

- Short-selling

- Lock-up periods

- Limits on shares issuable

Companies should know their investor.
A good advisor will help the company find the
appropriate investor and advise you on appropriate
protective provisions for your deal documents.

Short Selling

Investors are often criticized for short selling. It is assumed that if investors believe in a company enough to invest, then they should not be short selling. In some instances this is true. However, short selling a portion or all of the investment is a strategy utilized by some investors to mitigate, or hedge, the economic risk in their overall portfolio. While short selling *could* have a negative effect on a company, it is not, in and of itself, harmful to the company. Don't forget: for every buy transaction in a stock in the market, there is a corresponding sell transaction. Hedging activities do, however, need to be addressed in the company's discussions with the investor and any negotiated restrictions on short selling need to be incorporated into the purchase agreement with the investor. Essentially, there are three types of short-selling prohibitions:

- **Total prohibition on short selling.** With a total prohibition, the investor represents to the company that it has not been short the company's stock for a certain number of days prior to the closing and agrees not to go short until a specified number of days after.

- **No net-short provision.** A no net-short provision allows the investor to be short the company's shares, however the amount of shares short must be less than the amount that the investor is long at any given time, regardless of where and when the investor purchased the shares that it is holding long. This is a subtle distinction that is easy to overlook. If you are trying to prevent the investor from shorting your stock, a no net-short provision will not achieve this objective. When you are negotiating your deal documents, take the time to ensure that the language prohibiting shorting is what you bargained for in your discussions with the investor.

- **No selling in excess of the amount purchased in the transaction.** In this case, the investor is allowed to hedge some or all of the shares purchased in the transaction, but cannot be short more than the amount purchased in the financing. In contrast to the no net-short discussed above, this approach takes into account where and when the long shares were purchased.

There is one important caveat to keep in mind: a no net-short provision or other restriction on shorting or selling is contractual in nature— it is an agreement between the investor and the company. It has the full force and effect of contract law, but if the investor violates its agreement with the company and shorts anyway, there is no violation of the securities laws. The company will have the right to sue the investor for breach of contract for a violation of this provision, but lawsuits take time and money and damages have to be proven. The point is that companies should protect themselves contractually, such as with no net-short provisions, but really must also *know their investor*. A good advisor will help the company find the appropriate investor and advise you on the appropriate protective provisions for your deal.

Lock-Up Periods

A lock-up period, during which an investor cannot sell into the marketplace, is typically a contentious point to negotiate. Asking the investor to agree to a lock-up period requires the investor to assume additional risk that must be mitigated by providing the investor with additional potential for return or another means of reducing risk (for example, a price reset). Remember, one of the reasons to do a PIPE versus public offering is the ability of the company to negotiate transaction provisions tailored to meet the company's specific needs. A proper and appropriate lock-up period can take potential pressure off the company's stock for a certain period of time, and that lock-up has value for the company. Lastly, there is a relatively short *de facto* lock-up period on investor selling of the newly purchased shares until the time registration statement is declared effective and the shares can be resold in the public market. But that does not stop the investor from hedging through short-selling or otherwise during such period, unless otherwise agreed between the parties.

Cap on Number of Shares Issuable

For many reasons, it may be important or desirable to put a cap on the number of shares that can be issued upon conversion. Dilution is only one of them. In addition, NASD, NYSE, and AMEX rules limit the number of new shares that can be issued at a discount to under 20 percent without shareholder approval. Therefore, the parties may want to negotiate a "less-than 20 percent" cap. Also, 5 percent and 10 percent ownership thresholds trigger certain regulatory filing requirements for holders, so investors may want or need such a limitation.

On deals without hard floors, some hedge funds negotiate terms whereby in circumstances where more than 20 percent is issuable upon conversion (due to a precipitous price decline in the stock), then the company must either get shareholder approval to issue the additional shares or must redeem the securities for cash at the purchase price. A less common but far more onerous term is that if those first two provisions fail, the company must delist so that the investor is able to convert and sell its shares without violation of the applicable rules and regulations.

Pricing (Valuation)

Until now, we have focused on convertible structures, which offer the most complex (and flexible) set of features. We will now briefly focus on other forms of securities that can be used in a PIPE financing including common stock and warrants.

In the context of these instruments, the primary focus is on pricing (valuation) of the stock. How are PIPEs priced? First and foremost, pricing is an art, not a science. There is no mathematical black box where information can be entered at one end and a price pops out the other. The state of the general market, the specific industry, and the unique characteristics of the company all play a role. Moreover, each investor has its own unique risk-return profile. There are a number of generally accepted techniques for valuing a company's stock, but at the end of the day, pricing is the result of a negotiation process between the company and the investor. Here are some useful insights into the pricing the each of these types of securities in a PIPE transaction.

Common Stock Deals

Common stock PIPEs are generally priced at a discount to market price, with the amount of the discount depending upon the uncertainty

Pricing is an art, not a science.

surrounding the company's ability to achieve its future growth projections. Common stock investors realize a return on the investment as the company achieves milestones which increase the company's valuation and move the share price up. An investor who believes in the future of the company often prefers to buy in a private transaction because the purchase of a large block of stock in the open market can drive up the average purchase price.

In a common stock PIPE, the discount is not only driven by the business fundamentals of the company, but also to compensate for the lack of liquidity. Discounts range from a nominal discount to as high as 20 percent or more. While the discount is driven by the company's characteristics, industry, and market conditions, the ultimate discount is arrived at through negotiations between the investors and the company. An experienced financial advisor will be to advise you as to the appropriate discount for a company such as yours, given the general condition of the market and the specific terms of your transaction. Key factors are the length of time that the investor will be required to hold unregistered securities and other elements of the deal that may provide value to the investor (for example, price protection mechanisms and warrant coverage).

The investor will conduct an internal analysis to determine where the price needs to be set for the investor to achieve its desired rate of return for different pricing scenarios. The company and its advisors will need to guide the investor as to the prospects of the company and justify the price and terms that the company is seeking.

Warrants

A *warrant* is simply a piece of paper that gives the right to buy common stock at a certain price in the future. It is up to the holder of the warrant whether or not to execute that *option* at a future date. Issuing warrants as part of a transaction can increase upside potential, and thus be seen as a "sweetener" to make the deal more attractive to investors. The investor may in effect say to the company, "I understand what you're offering but that's just not enough for me given the risk profile of your company" or "At the end of day, if everything works out as planned, I'll

Cosmetically, a deal can look like a
common stock deal, but if it carries warrants
with a variable exercise price and no floor,
it becomes, in essence, a toxic or death spiral
convertible security.

be getting a 17 percent return on my money and I'm actually looking for 20 percent." By issuing warrants in connection with the deal, the issuer can offer the additional return required to offset perceived risk and secure that investor's capital.

Warrants can also be used to transform a fundamental deal into a technical deal. Cosmetically, a deal can look like a fundamental common stock deal, but if it carries warrants with a variable exercise price then the structure acts in a similar manner to a variable rate convertible deal. Without a floor, this instrument is strikingly similar to a toxic or death spiral convertible structure. However, a financially savvy company that insists on a common stock deal for appearances' sake, but cannot place a purely fundamental deal with investors, can carefully negotiate a common stock deal and use warrant coverage to entice the investor to participate in the transaction. The amount of warrant coverage offered by the company in a particular transaction depends upon the level of investor demand and the other terms of the transaction.

To summarize, a warrant is almost like a deal within a deal, in that all of its relevant features are subject to negotiation. In working with your advisor on any PIPE deal with warrants, you will need to determine how much value you are willing to give up in the transaction and negotiate the following:

- Warrant coverage (number of warrant shares per share purchased)

- Exercise price (price at which the underlying shares can be purchased)

- Term (period of time during which the warrant can be exercised)

- Registration rights (whether or not the shares underlying the warrant will be registered)

Two Key Conclusions

As with our previous chapter on PIPE deal structures, we want to leave you with two key conclusions as you emerge from the thicket of PIPE features:

A dose of reality up front
will save the company and its existing investors
tremendous heartache in the future.

- Be honest with yourself

- Don't attempt to be your own surgeon

Conclusion 1: Be Honest with Yourself

There is a tendency for management to be overly optimistic about the future prospects of their company. As a result, management often has unrealistic expectations about the value of the company's stock, and that is where the trouble begins. An experienced financial advisor will assist the company in analyzing the future potential of the company in order to put the company in the best possible light and achieve the best possible valuation in the transaction. In addition, your financial advisor can help you assess the impact of the financing structure on the company under different scenarios. A reality check today can save you much unnecessary grief in the future. Rather than taking a leap of faith and hoping everything turns out as planned, the company should work with its advisors to devise a structure that provides some wiggle room should the company's future performance not pan out exactly as anticipated. A dose of reality up front will save the company and its existing investors tremendous heartache in the future.

Conclusion 2: Don't Attempt to Be Your Own Surgeon

If there is one theme that should emerge from all this, especially from our discussion of convertible securities structures, it is the following: these instruments are incredibly flexible and complex and can do almost anything, *but they can also be extremely dangerous to the company if not used properly.* Understanding and dealing with the ramifications of these features can in and of itself be a full time job.

We don't think the answer is putting one's head in the sand and avoiding PIPES altogether just because of the *potential* risk. PIPEs are a highly effective financing alternative when used properly. When evaluating a PIPE financing for your company, keep the following in mind:

- The stronger your company's story, the more options that are available to you and the less likely that you will be forced to consider a deal with oppressive features (that is, you will be able to either do a fundamental deal or an attractively priced technical deal that is to your advantage—what we portrayed as the Sweet Spot in the FATE Model™ in Chapter 2).

- If your company's story is weaker and your options are limited to a technical PIPE, you still shouldn't shy away from considering a convertible security deal. We do, however, stress the importance of having a financial advisor who can help you understand the ramifications of the various features we discussed in this chapter and help you assess how they relate to one another in your specific transaction. In addition, your advisor can help you negotiate some of the terms to make the deal more palatable for you and the company.

As an analogy, we like to frame this discussion in terms of someone who is thinking about having elective surgery. On the one hand, you shouldn't let the fear of something going wrong keep you from all the benefits of the procedure. On the other hand, you wouldn't buy a scalpel and start performing the procedure on yourself. Even if you truly understood the surgical procedure, you wouldn't want to operate on yourself. You would conduct some preliminary research and find the names of some experienced, reputable surgeons that you could use to perform the procedure. You would interview these doctors to find the one you felt most comfortable with and in the process, you would find out what the potential dangers of the surgery, the outline of the overall procedure, the key qualifications of the surgeon, and so on. In short, you should take the time to get the right person for the job.

You are now armed with a wealth of knowledge regarding the fundamentals of PIPES, but you must still ask yourself if you truly understand all of the intricacies and ramifications of structuring a PIPE transaction. Even if you feel you do, you also need to ask yourself if it's really the best investment of your time to be sweating the details of a PIPE rather than running your company and helping create shareholder value. Your goal should be to find the best possible team of experts and advisors to help you move forward. Providing you with the information and tools to do that is the focus of our final chapter. We'll conclude the book with a discussion on choosing on a financial advisor who can help you make this kind of flexibility and complexity work for you as you move your company forward.

CHAPTER 5

GETTING DEALS DONE

T hroughout this book our goal has been to provide you with an insider's perspective on PIPEs. In the course of this journey, we have attempted to:

- Make you feel comfortable enough to evaluate the merits of PIPE financing for your company

- Dispel some of the most common misconceptions regarding PIPEs

- Teach you to think critically as you participate in each step of the PIPE process

- Provide a framework for understanding the difference between technical and fundamental deals and where your company fits

From this discussion we believe the following bottom line should emerge regarding PIPE deals in the real world: a PIPE can be a very effective weapon in the financing arsenal of your company, but when used inappropriately it can be very dangerous, even fatal.

A Question of Relationships

Even as we have tried to demystify much that is thought and said about PIPEs, we have also tried to show how the PIPEs world can be a complex and challenging place—not only because of the intrinsic difficulty of the subject matter, but also because no two PIPEs are ever exactly alike and because PIPE deal structures, features, and elements are by no means a fixed or stable landscape. Indeed, deal structures are constantly changing and shifting as new wrinkles are dreamed up and added to the mix by very skilled, intelligent players in this field. PIPEs aren't done in a vacuum—they aren't abstract, mathematical formulas found in books. Instead, they are always a *product of compromise*, which means working with people, developing relationships, and trying to create something that will be beneficial to all parties.

The PIPE relationship is a complex one in which you may—or may not—have common interests on any given issue with the investor before, during, and after the negotiation of the PIPE. In the middle we have a financial advisor whose duty is to serve your interests, but who must also work with the members of the investment community long after your PIPE is done. It's easy to see how this is a complex group dynamic with a number of actors and factors in play. In this chapter, we'd like to offer our experience working within this complex dynamic, in three areas:

- Selecting a financial advisor

- Selecting a legal advisor

- Understanding better the needs and issues of the investor

Selecting a Financial Advisor

In writing this book it has never been our intention to suggest you should go it alone when doing a PIPE (as we suggested at the end of Chapter 4, it is never a good idea to perform surgery on yourself regardless of how expert you may be). Expert advice is integral to a PIPE transaction if it is to be successful. This chapter focuses on how you should go about selecting the most appropriate financial advisor to get your deal done right.

We believe a critical element in the successful completion of a PIPE is the selection of your financial advisor. We'd go so far as to say that choosing the right advisors is crucial to the success of a PIPE and ultimately the success of your company. As we've noted, structuring a PIPE transaction improperly can be devastating to your company. Every PIPE is a uniquely structured transaction, which can be simple or extremely complex. Every element of a transaction is negotiable, but certain terms are more important than others to each of the parties in the transaction. The issuer needs to understand the interrelated aspects and the consequences of each of the elements, such as limits to dilution, issuance of warrants, the variable rate aspect of convertible securities, legal safe harbors, registration requirement exemptions, and other major aspects and potential effects of the deal. In order to negotiate effectively, the company must be sure its counsel, investment banker, and other advisors are expert and knowledgeable about PIPE transactions. It is a public company's obligation to review the transaction history and expertise of its advisors before entering into discussions to structure and execute a PIPE transaction.

That being said, *finding* such an advisor is easier said than done. This can be especially true as PIPEs become more and more commonplace as a financing option for companies. Not surprisingly, the choice of investment banks to advise issuers has grown tremendously of late. Formerly, only a few boutique investment banks specialized in PIPEs. As a result, these investment banks gained direct experience in a vast array of PIPE investing structures and experienced firsthand the successes and pitfalls of many structures and negotiated points in a transaction. Today the vast array of investment banks, including the bulge-bracket firms that once shunned the market, have become players. As such they may bring an impressive resume, client list, and pedigree to the table, but they may not bring much experience where it counts—in the world of actually structuring a wide variety of PIPE deals. In this marketplace, simply having a background in banking is not enough. The advisor must thoroughly know the ins and outs of the PIPE world, since the investors you'll be dealing with certainly will. And you never want an advisor who is learning on your dime, no matter how impressive the brand name on the letterhead.

This is especially true in the world of technical deals, where the investors involved work with these types of structures all the time. These investors may seem to be taking more of a risk with companies who are offering weaker stories, but this sense of risk is highly deceptive: these experienced, savvy investors are experts at building into deals every type of hedge to minimize the risk they actually face. Indeed, they are often taking even less risk than the investor dealing with the strong story of a fundamental deal with a strong company. If your financial advisor doesn't

Choosing the right advisor
is crucial to the success of a PIPE
and ultimately the success of your company.

understand the financial dynamics of this kind of situation, you can inadvertently get yourself in a bind by creating a deal that contains covenants that are difficult to live with and that place serious limits on any future transactions that you may want to do. (As an example of this, consider a deal where the investor builds in the right of first refusal for any follow-on deal you wish to do—and how that would handcuff you in soliciting new sources of funding.)

What you need then is a process to help you find a financial advisor who can do the best possible job for your company. We'll approach this by doing the following:

- Defining the role your financial advisor should play

- Giving you a set of questions that you should pose to each candidate for the role, along with some guidelines as to what to look for in their responses

Defining the Role of Your Financial Advisor

Finding a good advisor should begin with defining in your own mind the exact role you wish the advisor to play. From our experience, the investment banker has the following roles in every PIPE transaction:

- **Building a common language with you to help clarify where you want to go as a company.** This includes being able to identify the types of deal structures that are available and determining how your company fits in to that overall sense of structure. It then means identifying the particular deal structure that best suits you and providing you with a sense of the type of investor that is likely to participate in this type of deal.

- **Finding potential investors and matching the profiles of investors with the needs of the company.** This includes doing qualitative research on the investors that work in the framework and structure that you're interested in, identifying their mandate, and establishing the restrictions they must deal with, along with the amount of flexibility they can bring to any deal.

- **Working with the issuer and investors in the development of a structure.** This means creating a framework that is both appropriate to the company's situation and is fair and beneficial for all the parties in the transaction.

- **Guiding the company through the entire transaction process.** This means being there to help facilitate the process as a whole and deal with issues as they arise, with an eye to anticipating and resolving potential areas of conflict and clarifying areas of uncertainly as early as possible in the process.

Given this definition of the role your advisor should be playing, your next step is to begin interviewing the candidates. To help facilitate this, we have developed a list of questions that you should pose, along with what to listen for.

Asking the Right Questions

Conducting proper due diligence on a potential financial advisor is crucial. This means asking questions like, "How many PIPE deals have you completed?" and "Are PIPEs a new business line for you?" In Figure 10 we have summarized what we consider to be the Big 7 questions that you need to put to your potential advisor. We'll then walk through each question more detail.

Figure 10: Asking the Big 7 Questions

Question 1: What kind of experience does the financial advisor have doing PIPE transactions?

Question 2: Who will actually be working on your deal?

Question 3: How much do they know about your company?

Question 4: What range of deals might you expect from them?

Question 5: What is it going to cost?

Question 6: What does the PIPE process look like?

Question 7: What sort of relationship will you have with them?

Question 1: What kind of experience does the financial advisor have doing PIPE transactions? Not surprisingly, we have put this question right up front. As you make your journey through the world of PIPEs, you want an experienced professional who has traveled this road many times beforehand. There is no substitute for experience, not only in dealing with the big issues about deal structure but also in all the little nuances that come up as you negotiate the finer points of the deal. Of course, if you ask someone, "Are you experienced?" the likely reply will be, "But of course!" In posing this question you need to focus on the specifics and listen for a number of things in the advisor's replies, including *breadth* (the number of people in their organization who have worked with PIPES), *depth* (how long have they been doing PIPES), and *volume* (how many deals have they actually done). Here are a series of follow-up questions that you can use to drill down even further, although some of these questions will require that you talk to third parties and do some other independent research:

- Does the firm have extensive experience with PIPEs or is it turning to PIPEs just because other areas of investment banking have dried up or slowed down?

- What types of PIPEs has the firm arranged and closed? Are they comfortable doing both fundamental and technical deals? Or are they specialists in just one area? (If so, they may attempt to steer you into their comfort zone regardless of whether it's the right thing for you to do.)

- Has the firm successfully arranged PIPEs in your industry? In the issuing company's capitalization range? Of the type of structure being recommended?

- What is the track record of the PIPEs that they have done? What are the last ten deals they've completed? When did they do them? Are they a current, active player in the PIPE world? Who were the investors that bought the deals they worked on? What is their success ratio (that is, how many deals have they completed relative to the total number they have worked on)?

- What is the impression of the firm in the marketplace? What is the firm known for? Who are their references? (This also means asking questions of other management teams who have used what the advisor recommended once your interview with the advisor is over.)

- What is their record with the NASD? The SEC? Any black marks? If so, does this involve the principals of the firm? Brokers? Salesmen? (If the latter, it speaks to the issue of their judgment—that is, who they hire.)

Question 2: Who will actually be working on your deal? It's not uncommon in the opening, get-acquainted stage of the relationship to be wined, dined, and closed by a high-powered individual who has impeccable PIPE credentials, talks a great game, knows PIPEs cold, assures you that you will get the best possible service and support, shakes your hand firmly, gets you to sign on the dotted line, and then promptly . . . disappears! When you call the firm to start work on your deal, you realize that you are actually partnered with a junior associate, a freshly minted MBA straight out of business school, who is just beginning a career in this field. You need to make sure that all those reassuring answers that you received in response to Question 1 actually relate to the people you'll be dealing with. This is also a good way to test the potential advisor's veracity and trustworthiness. It's easy to give a canned presentation about corporate capabilities and world-class service, but execution is key. Finally, one more key thing to look for involves asking the advisor, "Will you be available for advice concerning the transaction after the deal has closed?" This is especially useful if the stock should slip somewhat and advice might be of special value.

Question 3: How much do they know about your company? At this point you've asked the potential advisor, "How well do you know the subject of PIPEs?" Once you've established their PIPE expertise, your next line of questioning should be, "How well do you know me and my company?" This is the "Have you done your homework?" question. At your first meeting, the advisor may run a wonderful dog-and-pony show about their own capabilities, but when it comes to your company, suddenly they may deal in nothing more than high-level generalities If they haven't taken the time to learn about your company while they are trying to win your business, what are they likely to do once you've signed them up? The likelihood is that they will be giving you a generic, one-size-fits-all approach. Since this is an important transaction for your company and you are paying for advisory services, you deserve an advisor that views you as an important client.

Question 4: What range of deals might you expect from them? As the potential advisor lays out an overall approach to the PIPE process, it is a natural transition to also ask the financial advisor to give you a broad-brush picture of what kind of deal structures you might reasonably expect to be dealing with. We are not talking about a fully developed proposal for a course of action. If the advisor knows PIPES and has done the required degree of homework on your company, it is not at all unreasonable to start the process of thinking about where you would go from here. How can you make a final decision if you don't know what you are hiring the advisor to do? In asking this, you will accomplish a number of things. You will give yourself a quick reality check based on your own assumptions and understanding of where your company is and the options that are available, and you'll also get a snapshot of how the advisor thinks about PIPEs. You can use the following questions to probe for more detail:

- What investors are they recommending? Do they have relationships with the investors?

- Do they have ongoing relationships with the investors that can help them to identify the most appropriate investors for your situation?

- What are the profiles of the targeted investors? Are they fundamental or technical players? Are they knowledgeable about your company and industry? Do the investors tend to hold stocks for an extended period or "flip" out of them quickly?

Question 5: What is it going to cost? Naturally, you have every right to ask what the advisor expects to charge for services, as well as how those fees will be structured in relation to the deal itself. Your goal here is to determine whether their fees are in line with reasonable and standard fees for the industry. In this book, we can't describe what those fees should be—they are driven by both market and transaction-specific factors—but with a little bit of research and some comparison shopping, you should be able to quickly determine the reasonableness of your fee quotes. The bottom line here, of course, involves knowing how the fees work, knowing exactly what you're getting for your money, and feeling comfortable that you are getting an equitable deal.

Question 6: What does the overall PIPE process look like? In this book, we have laid out a process for understanding and creating a PIPE, and in doing so we have spelled out our overall philosophy of how PIPEs should work and how to think about them. We're not saying, of course, that this is the only way that one can think about the subject—every financial advisor will have their own approach to how a PIPE deal should be done. What are the key steps in the process? Which ones form the critical path to successful execution of the deal? What is the anticipated timing from engagement of the advisor to the closing of the transaction?

Question 7: What kind of relationship can you have with them? As you work through these questions with a would-be financial advisor, you should be evaluating your ability to communicate with the advisor. We're talking here about the whole process of defining the give and take that lies at the heart of any relationship. Do you feel the advisor is listening to you? Is the advisor responding with canned, formulaic answers or really taking into account who you are and what you're saying? Is the advisor open to your ideas? Or has the advisor already come to a conclusion regardless of your input? Is the advisor willing to truly work with you to clearly explain your options and help you to effectively evaluate the alternatives?

Selecting a Legal Advisor

We are confident our readers already know that there is no substitute for expert legal advice in business. This maxim is doubly true in the complex world of PIPEs. Let us offer a short list of questions a CEO should know the answers to before selecting a PIPEs lawyer:

- Does the prospective attorney work on securities transactions for public companies? Has the attorney worked on PIPEs before? Which deals? How long ago? What kind of structure? Who were the investors? This will tell a lot about what kind of deal it was. Was there an agent involved? Who was it?

- Is the attorney up to speed on the newest pronouncements from the SEC, the newest PIPE structures, the newest version of PIPEs purchase agreements, so that he or she can anticipate all of the pieces that go into getting the deal done? It is likely to hurt the company if the lawyer is busy coming up to speed in these areas when the prospective investors know them cold. Does the attorney regularly work on and submit filings to the SEC? Does he or she understand and regularly deal with the commission on where the issues are likely to be? Also, does the attorney understand potential NASD issues and how to navigate through the NASD, when necessary?

- Is the attorney practical rather than theoretical? Does the attorney have a good business sense and is he or she able to explain the legal risks from a business perspective so the CEO can make an informed business decision about what is important and what is OK to give in on? Is the attorney a strong negotiator?

- Does the attorney know how to best protect the company when it comes to issues like short sales and other hedging techniques and deal with issues such as the resale of technically restricted securities and how to work with transfer agents?

- Does the attorney typically represent issuers or investors? Who else does the attorney represent (both the individual attorney and the firm)? Check references and talk to others who have used this lawyer to make sure you'll get what you think you are getting.

- Does the attorney have the ability to get the deal done quickly and competently, avoiding the "overlawyering" that can undermine the goodwill and interest of investors?

Once again, we cannot understate the importance of sound, experienced legal advice in putting together a PIPE deal. Be certain to select a legal advisor who is right for the job.

Thinking about the Investor

In discussing how to select a financial advisor, we introduced the idea that your advisor should be talking with you early in the process about the types of investors he or she might think appropriate for your company. In your role as informed participant in the PIPE process, it is vital that you work actively with your advisor to select the most appropriate investors for your company, and not simply hand this matter over to the "expert." You should never simply accept investors blindly.

In short, there is one point that we cannot stress strongly enough: You should know who your investors are going to be. If the deal involves more than one investor, you should know the composition of the investor group. This is critical because of the simple adage that not all money is created equal. At first blush this may seem nonsensical: Money is money is money. In pure dollar amounts, that is true, but whenever you think of getting money you need to think not just of the amount you will receive but also about all the terms, conditions, and attachments that may come along with it. If your advisor refuses to involve you and keeps you in the dark about this, you should consider it a serious red flag and re-evaluate whether this is the right advisor to be involved with.

So what issues should you and your advisor be considering when screening and auditioning investors? Naturally, in thinking about dealing with any investor, one quick question should immediately come to mind: Why does this person or entity want to invest in your company? Is it because they know your industry? Do they have other investments in the industry? Or is it because they are happy with the deal structure and the protections it offers them—that is, are they essentially a technical investor? A good clue here can be the amount of due diligence the investor actually does on your company. If they ask all of their questions in twenty minutes and decide to move forward with an investment, it's probably a sign they really aren't that interested in your company. How could they be? They haven't spent the time.

Conversely, there are a number of issues and questions that you need to investigate as you perform your own due diligence about the investor:

- If you are dealing with a fund, what is its charter? Is its focus short or long term? Does it follow a "buy and hold" strategy? Is it a hedge fund using both long and short positions in order to better manage risk?

- What is their reputation? In this context, we're not speaking just in terms of their sector expertise, but also of their integrity and in the way they interact with companies. Get references and talk to your peers at the other companies regarding their experience dealing with the investor. How did they behave when things took a turn for the worse? It is important to understand how the investor reacts both when things go well and when they don't go quite so well.

- What might one investor bring to the table compared to another (besides just money)? For example, the involvement of a highly sophisticated, greatly respected investor may in and of itself send a signal to the market that increases your company's valuation. In another instance, a given investor might give you access to other strategic relationships and connections that could be very positive for your company. In short, who do they know? And will they introduce you?

The early courtship stages of this relationship are also significant in that this is the period where everyone is on their best behavior. Given that you're seeing the investor at their best, it's a good time to evaluate your gut instincts, such as: Do you relate to them? Can you talk to them? Do you like them? Does their management style work for you? This is especially true if the investor wishes to be actively involved in your company.

Beyond these questions, there is another key point to keep in mind. Sometimes your interests and those of the investor will be aligned; at other times they will be completely divergent. At first this idea may be seem to contradict common sense. After all, the goal of the issuing company is to protect shareholder value, while the goal of the investor is to enjoy the benefits of being a shareholder; it would seem you should both be in alignment. The reality, however, is that management is entrusted to protect shareholder value for all shareholders, and the individual PIPE investor's interests may not always be aligned with those of the other shareholders.

To illustrate this point, consider the following scenario. Company and Investor do a fundamental deal based on Company's strong story. The deal structure is entirely common stock. Investor buys the stock at $3 a share. Both sides very much want the value of the stock to appreciate. Thus their interests are in complete alignment. Time goes by and the stock price declines. Now Company needs to raise more money based on a stock evaluation of $2 per share. Investor, for obvious reasons, doesn't care for this plan. Instead, he advises holding out for another six months with the hopes of weathering the storm. Company replies, "We need that money now to survive. And 90 percent of our shareholders bought their stock at $1 per share so they will still be happy." Because interests sometimes diverge, it is critical that management be able to maintain an open line of communication with its investors to resolve conflicts as quickly and painlessly as possible.

A Final Thought

We began this book with a simple story in which we tried to express the personal, devastating impact that can result from not being able to find the proper kind of financing for a company. In short, we've been there. We felt, first-hand, the pain of watching a company slip away that we created, built up, and made flourish, due to the lack of a flexible form of financing like a PIPE. We would argue that it is exactly this level of comprehension that comes from experience—the ability to truly sense *why* companies are looking for financing—that makes the difference between the extraordinary financial advisor and the merely competent. It's a matter of understanding, empathy, and accessibility. In securing a PIPE, you deserve nothing less than that from your advisor.

Above all though, we want our final word to you to be one of encouragement. As the old adage goes, "You can't win if you aren't in the game." Assemble the best team of advisors you can and then go out and make it happen. Be sure to apply the guidelines and take the precautions that we have laid out in this book. We are confident that you will find PIPEs a wonderfully responsive, flexible, and innovative financial tool to help you grow your company and accomplish your objectives.

APPENDIX

A SHORT HISTORY OF SECURITIES LAW

Securities law is an integral part of every PIPE transaction. A firm understanding of the nature of and reasoning behind this law is essential for all executive officers of public companies considering PIPE transactions to ensure compliance with the intent and the technicalities of the law. This chapter provides a short history of the Securities Act of 1933 and Securities Exchange Act of 1934 and the evolution of the basic law of private placements and PIPEs, necessary exemptions from registration and prospectus delivery requirements, various safe harbors for original issuances and resales, and an understanding of the important—and potentially confusing—doctrine of integration.[1]

Genesis of the '33 and '34 Acts

The Great Stock Market Crash of 1929 rocked the nation. During the Roaring Twenties approximately 20 million people took advantage of postwar prosperity and sought new fortunes in the stock market.[2] $50 billion of new securities were issued in the United States during the decade following World War I. When the market crashed in 1929, half of these securities proved to be worthless, and the fortunes of countless investors were lost.[3] Since banks had also heavily invested in the markets, people feared that their banks would not be able to pay back their deposits, so runs on banks succeeded the stock market crash, causing numerous bank failures. The Great Depression ensued.

With the Crash and Depression, public confidence in the markets plummeted. Congress held hearings on why the crash occurred and how to restore public faith in the markets. A House committee report found numerous securities to have been fraudulently sold by underwriters and dealers without "standards of fair, honest, and prudent dealing" and without any real information by which investors could actually evaluate the merits of the securities. Prior to the Crash, securities regulations were the domain of the states. Based on the findings of the Congressional

---

[1] This chapter is in no way intended to replace the advice of legal counsel, nor be inclusive of all the legal matters that issuers must contend with. An issuer should rely on its own legal counsel to deal with the intricacies of the laws, rules and regulations. Expert advice from both your legal counsel and investment banker on a particular transaction has no substitute.

[2] www.sec.gov/about/whatwedo.

[3] www.sec.gov/about/whatwedo.

The main purposes of the '33 and '34 Acts are full and fair disclosure by companies offering securities to the public.

hearings, Congress passed the Securities Act of 1933 (the "'33 Act") and the Securities Exchange Act of 1934 (the "'34 Act"), thereby assigning primary, uniform regulation of securities and the securities markets to the federal government, supplemented by individual states' laws. The main purposes of the '33 and '34 Acts are full and fair disclosure by companies offering securities to the public. People who sell and trade securities—brokers, dealers and exchanges—must treat investors fairly and honestly, putting investors' interests first.

Often referred to as the "truth in securities" law, the Securities Act of 1933 has one basic objective: full and fair disclosure of the merits and risks of securities. The key elements of the '33 Act are: 1) mandatory full disclosure issued to the public in a filed registration statement, 2) SEC review of the registration statement in order to deem the registration "effective" so that sales could commence, 3) mandatory delivery of a prospectus to purchasers and offerees, and 4) civil liabilities for untrue statements and material omissions and violations of registration requirements.

With the Securities Exchange Act of 1934, Congress created the Securities and Exchange Commission and empowered the SEC with broad authority over all aspects of the securities industry. This included the power to register, regulate, and oversee brokerage firms and the nation's stock exchanges and self-regulatory organizations, like the NASD. The '34 Act also prohibited certain types of conduct in the markets and provided the Commission with disciplinary powers over regulated entities and persons associated with them. Moreover, the '34 Act empowered the SEC to require periodic reporting of information by companies with publicly traded securities.

The crux of the '33 Act is that all offers and sales of securities in the United States using interstate commerce or the mails must comply with the registration and prospectus delivery requirements of Section 5 of the '33 Act, absent an applicable exemption. As all senior officers of public companies know, registration can be costly and time-consuming.

Absent an applicable exemption,
all offers and sales of securities
in the United States using interstate commerce
or the mails must comply with the registration
and prospectus delivery requirements
of Section 5 of the '33 Act.

The Exemptions

Over the years the SEC has developed alternative exemptions and safe harbors that can enable an issuer to raise capital and issue securities more quickly and less expensively than a registered offering. Exemptions can be related either to the type of securities or the nature of the transaction in which the securities were issued. The burden of proving the applicability of the exemption is on the person claiming it. For issuers, a faulty exemption can be disastrous. If securities issued pursuant to a purported exemption are deemed to be truly a public offering or part of a public offering, a violation of the '33 Act will have occurred and the buyers of the securities can demand their money back for a year after issuance (they essentially are granted an irrevocable "put" on the issuer).

Section 3 of the '33 Act exempts certain securities from the registration requirements and Section 4 exempts certain transactions, such as private placements. Section 4(1) exempts all transactions by any person other than an issuer, underwriter, or a dealer. Although it seems clear who is covered by this exemption and who is not, one can be deemed a "statutory underwriter" and therefore ineligible to use this exemption.[5] However, it is Section 4(1) that allows an ordinary person to buy and sell 100 shares on a listed exchange, through NASDAQ, or in the over-the-counter markets, without violating the registration requirements of the '33 Act.

Section 4(2) exempts transactions by an issuer not involving a public offering. This is essentially the main exemption for "private placements." The securities issued under this exemption are so-called "restricted securities," the implications of which are discussed below.

Reselling of Restricted Securities

Unlike the owner of an exempt or registered security, which is freely tradable in both public and private transactions (assuming no contractual restrictions), an owner of restricted securities—securities acquired in a

---

[5] §2(11): The term "underwriter" means any person who has purchased from an issuer with a view to, or offers or sells for an issuer in connection with, the distribution of any security, or participates or has a direct or indirect participation in any such undertaking, or participates or has a participation in the direct or indirect underwriting of any such undertaking.

A faulty exemption can be disastrous for an issuer.

private placement—must find an exemption or safe harbor, or must register such securities in order to dispose of them. There are generally six ways that an owner of private placement, or restricted, securities can dispose of such securities:

1. In a registered offering

2. In a further private placement

3. To the public in a transaction not involving a "distribution" pursuant to the provisions of Rule 144, which limit the amount, manner of sale, and minimum holding period for such securities to be sold

4. To "qualified institutional buyers" ("QIBs") who purchase for their own account or that of another QIB, pursuant to Rule 144A

5. In an offshore transaction under the resale provisions of Regulation S

6. Freely, pursuant to Rule 144(k), if the owner is a nonaffiliate of the issuer and has held the securities for two years in compliance with such rule.

In a typical PIPE transaction, a resale registration statement is filed by the issuer on behalf of the purchasers. However, technical SEC rules and regulations regarding private placements, appropriate exemptions, and integration safe harbors (addressed below) must be carefully adhered to in each case to avoid a violation of the securities laws by the issuer.

The Private Placements Exemption

As stated above, Section 4(2) of the '33 Act exempts from the registration and prospectus delivery requirements of Section 5 all "transactions by an issuer not involving any public offering." This is the "private placements" exemption. As with other exemptions from Section 5's requirements, the burden is on the issuer to prove that the exemption is available for the particular transaction; Section 12(a)(1) of the '33 Act gives the purchaser the right to rescind the transaction for one year following the sale if a violation of the registration requirements occurs.

Section 4(2) exempts transactions by an issuer not involving a public offering. This is essentially the "private placements" exemption.

Unfortunately, Congress did not initially provide guidance as to what factors would be used to determine whether an offering was a "public offering." Each situation was judged on its own facts, which naturally provided much uncertainty in the marketplace. Initially the SEC focused on the number of offerees, with the number becoming 25 by 1935, but this was not by itself dispositive of the issue. The SEC cited other principal factors, including the relationship of the offerees to the issuer (were they in such a relationship as to have special knowledge of the issuer?), the number of units offered (a few units would be more indicative of a non-public offering than many units), the size of the offering (the smaller, the better), and the manner of offering (if the issuer was communicating directly with purchasers, there would be more likely a determination of a non-public offering). "Investment intent" was also introduced as a factor, but even with this guidance, the SEC stressed that each situation would be judged on its own merits, and for many years issuers and their counsel were at a loss for definitive guidelines. Number tests seemed to be the emphasis for decades.

In 1953 the U.S. Supreme Court's decision in *S.E.C. v. Ralston Purina Co.* shifted the emphasis from numbers to the ability of the offerees to fend for themselves.[6] In *Ralston,* the manufacturer of mixed feeds for poultry and livestock and cereal for humans had offered stock ownership to employees who could meet its test of "key employees." Any employee, from manager to chow loading foreman to clerical assistant, was eligible to become a "key employee" and be able to buy company stock at a discount. From 1947 through 1950, more than a thousand employees purchased such stock at discounted prices as part of Ralston's bonus and loyalty program. The District Court hearing the case sympathized with Ralston management's intent and held that the private offering exemption had been satisfied. This holding was affirmed by the Court of Appeals. But the Supreme Court disagreed. Justice Clark, in a landmark decision, stated that the applicability of the private offering exemption should turn on "whether the particular class of persons affected

---

[6] *S.E.C. v. Ralston Purina Co.*, 346 U.S. (1953)

The burden is on the issuer to prove that the exemption is available for the particular transaction; the '33 Act gives the purchaser the right to rescind the transaction for one year following the sale if a violation the registration requirements occurs.

needs the protection of the Act." The basic test, in his opinion, was whether the offerees were "able to fend for themselves." Clark rejected a numbers test, stating that "the statute would seem to apply to a 'public offering' whether to few or many." Thus the strict number test was gone and replaced by a test of the ability of the offerees.

The next major development of the private offering exemption occurred with the publication of the SEC's comments in 1957 of its investigation of a purported private placement of convertible debentures by the Crowell-Collier Publishing Company.[7] Two major themes developed from this case. First, a series of related transactions cannot be separated in order to establish that a particular part is a private transaction if, taken as a whole, it is a public offering. Second, the previous one-year rule of thumb became a two-year rule of thumb that was generally applied by the securities bar when advising its clients regarding resales of securities initially issued in a private placement.

In 1962, the SEC addressed the doctrine of "changed circumstances," which was then an important consideration in determining when resales could take place. The SEC took the position that an unforeseen change of circumstances since the date of purchase of securities could constitute the basis of an opinion that a proposed resale of securities is not inconsistent with an original "investment intent" representation. Fluctuations in stock price, however, were not to be considered an acceptable claim of changed circumstances. In addition, the SEC also rehashed a number of previously stated positions, namely that whether a transaction is one not involving any public offering is essentially a question of fact and necessitates a consideration of all surrounding circumstances, including such factors as the relationship between the offerees and the issuer, and the nature, scope, size, type and manner of the offering. Issuers and their counsel were still left in the dark as to specific guidelines.

Finally, in 1972, the SEC adopted Rule 144, which brought objective standards to the question of resales of privately placed securities. Under

---

[7] SEC Release No 33-3825, August 12, 1957

For many years issuers and their counsel
were at a loss for definitive guidelines.

Rule 144, a nonaffiliated holder of restricted securities could sell limited amounts in a prescribed fashion after two years, through a broker and upon filing notice with the SEC. Rule 144 has since been amended, and today nonaffiliates can sell limited amounts in a prescribed fashion after only one year, with unlimited sales after two years.

In the 1970s, a number of judicial decisions were made that appeared to limit the availability of the Section 4(2) exemption. Under pressure from the financial community, the SEC adopted Rule 146, which provided a safe harbor for reliance on the private placement exemption. Rule 146 was designed to create greater certainty in the application of the Section 4(2) exemption.[8] Like Reg D today, the private placement exemption in Rule 146 would be available to issuers if specified conditions were met relating to the manner of the offering, the nature of the offerees and purchasers, access to or furnishing of information, limitations on the number of purchasers, and procedures designed to limit subsequent resales. In light of the mixed opinions regarding Rule 146, in 1981 the SEC proposed that the rule be superseded by a new Regulation D.

Today's Private Placement Vehicle

Reg D was adopted in 1982. Since then it has been refined and improved, and continues today to operate as an important safe harbor under Section 4(2). Reg D is the principal private offering exemption under U.S. securities laws.

As written today, Reg D comprises Rules 501 through 506 of the '33 Act and provides several key exemptions from registration. Principally useful for small companies, Rules 504 (for nonreporting companies) and 505 provide exemptions from registrations under Section 3(b) for offerings no great than $1 million and $5 million, respectively. Rule 506, however, is the '33 Act's principal private placement exemption pursuant to 4(2) for offerings of unlimited amounts and is focused on here.

Rules 501 through 503 apply to all of the Reg D exemptions. Rule 501

---

[8] *S.E.C. v. Ralston Purina Co.*, 346 U.S. (1953)

"… an issuer or an underwriter may not separate parts of a series of related transactions comprising an issue of securities of related transactions and thereby seek to establish that a particular part is a private transaction if the whole really involves a public offering."

defines key terms for Reg D, including "accredited investor." The term is defined to include virtually every type of institution that participates in the private placement market as well as individuals with substantial net income or net worth (generally, $200,000 per year net income or $1 million net worth). Rule 502 provides a key safe harbor from "integration" for offerings completed six months before or commenced six months after other securities offerings of the same class. The doctrine of *integration* enables the SEC to view a private offering as part of (that is, integrated with) another past, present, or future offering of securities by an issuer if such offerings are deemed by the SEC to be truly parts of one unified offering. If a private offering is integrated with a public offering, then the private offering exemption will be lost and a '33 Act violation will occur. This doctrine of integration is thus an important concept for private placement exemptions and is discussed more fully in the next section. Pursuant to Rule 503, a form D notice of the Reg D private placement must be filed with the SEC within 15 days after the first sale.

Rule 506, the key exemption, has no dollar limit for the offering, and the offering can be made to up to 35 nonaccredited investors and unlimited accredited investors. Specified information must be given to nonaccredited offerees but there are no special information disclosure requirements required for accredited investors. Significantly, no offer or sales can be made by any form of "general solicitation" nor general advertising. This requirement applies to the issuer or anyone acting on its behalf (such as a placement agent or investment bank).

Securities sold pursuant to Reg D, as all securities issued in exempt transactions, are "restricted" under the securities laws and must have a legend or other "reasonable assurance" to the issuer that that shares will be resold only in compliance with applicable rules. Securities issued under Reg D may therefore only be resold if the subsequent sale meets another exemption or the sale has been registered with the SEC.

The Danger of Integration

Since adoption of the '33 Act, a burning issue with respect to exemptions, especially those pursuant to Section 4(2), has been whether a pri-

Reg D is the principal private offering exemption under U.S. securities laws.

vate offering would be viewed as part of (that is, *integrated* with) another past, present, or future offering of securities by the issuer. The danger is that the other offering would be a public offering and, since the private offering would not have been registered, a violation of the '33 Act's registration and prospectus delivery requirements would then have occurred, although accidentally. In addition, two or more private offerings could be integrated and deemed a "public offering." With the investors' right to rescission upon violation of registration and prospectus delivery requirements (no questions asked), *either* could be disastrous for the issuer and its other investors.

If a private offering is integrated with a public offering or two or more private offerings are integrated and deemed a public offering, a violation of the '33 Act will result.

The Five-Factor Test

In 1962, the SEC issued the so-called Five-Factor Test to provide guidance on the integration of completed offerings. The following factors were deemed to be determinative of whether two or more transactions should be integrated and deemed as one:

1. Are the offerings part of a single plan of financing?

2. Do they have the same general purpose?

3. Are the offerings of the same class of security?

4. Are they being made at or about the same time?

5. Are the securities being sold for the same type of consideration?

These factors became codified in Reg D in 1982, and the Five-Factor Test continues to be used today. Reg D provided an important new safe harbor from integration for private offerings pursuant to Reg D and public offerings six months apart. But the test created more questions than it answered. First, the SEC's interpretations of the Five-Factor Test were very fact-specific, so that guiding precedence was not established. Second, only

If a private offering is integrated with a public offering or two or more private offerings are integrated and deemed a public offering, a violation of the '33 Act will result.

one or two of the factors could be determinative of the issue, but priorities were not indicated by the SEC.

In 1986, in a No-Action Letter to *Verticom, Inc.*, the SEC surprisingly did not utilize the Five-Factor Test and instead applied Rule 152 to determine not to integrate a *completed* private offering with a subsequent proposed public offering within six months. Rule 152, the original integration safe harbor, has remained essentially unchanged since its adoption in 1935, and reads: "The phrase 'transactions by an issuer not involving any public offering' in Section 4(2) shall be deemed to apply to transactions not involving any public offering at the time of said transactions although subsequently thereto the issuer decides to make a public offering and/or files a registration statement."

Thus it might seem that, according to this Rule, validly exempt completed private offerings would not be integrated with later public offerings. However, the adopting release for Rule 152 stated that the purpose of Rule 152 was more limited than would appear on first blush: that *only failed or uncompleted offerings would be protected.* This safe harbor has not been definitively interpreted by the SEC and the securities bar had not given it much attention until *Verticom.*[9] Rule 152 then became the classic safe harbor, protecting *completed* private offerings from being integrated with a later public offering. But when is an offering deemed completed? And can a private offering and public offering ever be simultaneous without them being integrated? In 1990 and 1992, these questions were answered to some extent.

In 1990, in the now famous *Black Box* No-Action Letter, the SEC deemed that a private offering was "completed" (for purposes of integration) when a purchase agreement has been fully executed and the consideration and commitment on behalf of the purchaser in the private offering are subject only to conditions outside of the control of the investors. Thus an issuer could then file a registration statement covering the resale of the securities issued in the private offering, even if the securities had not yet been fully issued and paid for. For the first time, Rule 152 began to

---

[9]   Verticom, Inc. No-Action Letter, Jan. 1986 (Letter to the SEC).

The doctrine of *integration* enables the SEC to view a private offering as part of (that is, integrated with) another past, present, or future offering of securities by an issuer if such offerings are deemed by the SEC to be truly parts of one, unified offering.

have real teeth. *Black Box* made it clear, however, that renegotiation of the terms of the purchase agreement after the filing of the registration statement could constitute a new offering and could therefore be integrated.

The second landmark ruling in *Black Box* concerned a simultaneous public and private offering to a limited number of qualified offerees. Specifically, the SEC allowed a private placement of convertible securities commenced *after* filing of a public registration statement to a limited number of purchasers to not be integrated. In a follow-up clarifying No-Action Letter, *Squadron Ellenoff,* the SEC specifically noted that this position taken in *Black Box* was to be narrowly construed to the facts given, specifically that the offering was made solely to 1) institutions that would be Qualified Institutional Buyers for purposes of Rule 144A (described below) and 2) no more than two or three large institutional accredited investors. Hence, *Black Box* also became known for its limited qualified institutional buyer exemption, which would allow a simultaneous, or side-by-side, public offering and private offering to certain qualified institutional buyers.

Squadron Ellenoff also clarified the SEC's position on convertible securities: the SEC treats an offering of a class of securities and an offering of another security convertible into that class of securities to be the same for purposes of the integration doctrine. Thus, a private offering of convertible debentures that are convertible into common stock would be deemed to be an offering of the underlying common stock and therefore potentially integratable into a public offering of common stock under the five-factor test. This was a very important clarification for PIPEs in which convertible debt, convertible preferred stock or warrants are issued.

While *Black Box* and *Squadron Ellenoff* added some more clarity to the integration doctrine, questions were still unanswered for the securities bar, such as failed/abandoned offerings. These questions and others had a chilling effect on private placements as attorneys were not certain as to how to properly advise their clients.

In 1998, the SEC acknowledged that the then-current integrations doctrine had resulted in uncertainty for issuers and had significantly

Rule 152 then became the classic safe harbor, protecting completed private offerings from being integrated with a later public offering.

restricted issuers' ability to switch between public and private offerings. In its so-called Aircraft Carrier Release, the SEC proposed several amendments to then-current Rule 152 to allow issuers more flexibility by providing safe harbors that 1) allow a *completed or abandoned* private offering to be followed by a public offering and 2) allow a private offering to be commenced after abandonment of a registered public offering.

But with respect to the "public to private" safe harbor, the additional flexibility would come at a price: if the securities were first offered in the private offering within 30 days after abandonment of the public offering, the issuer and underwriters would have to agree in writing to accept Section 11 and Section 12(a)(2) liability for the offering documents used in the private offering (this would impose a greater liability standard on the issuer and underwriters in the private offering than the Rule 10b-5 liability standard that was found by the U.S. Supreme Court to apply to unregistered transactions).

The Aircraft Carrier Proposal also proffered no further guidance concerning the general integration doctrine, nor proposals regarding "side-by-side" public and private offerings, even where all investors in the private were QIBs and there has been no general solicitation. In such cases, the *Black Box, Squadron Ellenoff,* and other No-Action Letters would still continue to provide the only available SEC guidance if the Aircraft Carrier amendments to Rule were adopted as proposed, which they ultimately were not.

The Final Rules on Integration

In January 2001, the SEC discarded the Aircraft Carrier proposals and passed final rules on integration, creating a new Rule 155 which provides for a safe harbor only for a registered offering following an abandoned private offering or a private offering following an abandoned publicly registered offering. An issuer can now first determine what kind of interest it may have in a private offering or public offering before switching to the other format, if the rules are adhered to (but only if the original offering is totally abandoned and no securities were sold).

Black Box deemed that a private offering was "completed" (for purposes of integration) when a purchase agreement has been fully executed and the consideration and commitment on behalf of the purchaser in the private offering are subject only to conditions outside of the control of the investors.

Pursuant to new Rule 155, an abandoned or terminated private offering can be changed into a public offering and not be integrated if no securities were sold in the private offering, all offering activity in the private offering is terminated before the registration statement is filed; and any prospectus filed as part of the registration statement discloses specified information about the abandoned private offering. If any securities in the private offering were offered to non-accredited investors or investors were not "sophisticated," then the public offering filing must wait 30 days. For an initially registered offering to be changed to a private offering and not be integrated, the private offering must not commence until 30 days after the effective date of withdrawal of the registration statement, no securities can have been sold in the registered offering, and certain disclosures must be made in the private offering, including that a registration statement had been filed and withdrawn.

Integration of public offerings can be disastrous for the issuer and existing investors. The existing morass of rules, exemptions, and safe harbors have come to be known as the Metaphysics of Integration, and while they are too numerous to fully elaborate upon here they are a critically important consideration when undertaking a PIPE. The above discussion is intended only to give you the history of the doctrine, its numerous incantations and some of the key current rules. Companies and investors should arm themselves with advisors who can guide them through the muck to determine the rules applicable to their situation.

It has been said that the field of institutionalized private placements has been "revolutionized" since 1990 by Rule 144A, which provides a *resale* safe harbor for certain persons *other than issuers* to resell certain securities they have purchased directly or indirectly from the issuer in a private offering to "qualified institutional buyers" (QIBs). Under Rule 144A, buyers of privately placed securities that are not also listed on exchanges or quoted on NASDAQ can resell them to QIBs without the need for a registration statement, thus providing another avenue of liquidity for PIPE investors.

A QIB is a specified type of institution, acting on its own or on behalf of other QIBs, that in the aggregate owns and invests on a discretionary basis at least $100 million in securities of issuers that are not related with

Under Rule 144A, buyers of privately placed securities that are not also listed on exchanges or quoted on NASDAQ can resell them to QIBs without the need for a registration statement, thus providing another avenue of liquidity for PIPE investors.

the entity. Notably, there is no prohibition in Rule 144A against "general solicitation."

Reg S—Safe Harbor for Securities Issued Offshore

In 1990, the SEC adopted Reg S to provide clear guidelines as to when securities issued outside the United States were required to be registered with the SEC. Without Reg S, theoretically, any securities offering to the public, anywhere in the world, would be subject to Section 5's registration requirements. It was not long before Reg S was discovered as a boon for small equity offerings offshore.

To many small cap issuers and investment bankers, Reg S offered a speedy, low-cost way for U.S. companies to issue privately placed securities at deep discounts offshore, which could then be resold in the United States after 40 days without registration. Although this was not necessarily the intent of the SEC, this practice burgeoned. European investors rarely demanded managerial control; there was then not an equivalent European NASDAQ market where European investors could invest in small, growing, dynamic high tech companies, and Europeans tended to do little, if any, active due diligence on the Reg S companies before investing. Reg S also did not contain the same disclosure requirements of Reg D, and thus Reg S became a speedy, cost-effective way of raising much capital. Reg S generally provides that any offer or sale that occurs within the United States is subject to Section 5, while an offer or sale that occurs outside the United States is not.

Reg S contains two general conditions to ensure that securities in fact "come to rest" offshore. Under the first condition, "offshore transactions," no offers or sales can be made to persons in the United States and either the buyer must be outside the United States at origination of the buy or the transaction must be executed using the facilities of a foreign exchange (and not be pre-arranged with anyone in the United States). Under the second general condition, a prohibition of "directed selling efforts" in the United States, activities are prohibited that are intended or should be expected to result in a conditioning of a market in the United States for the securities being placed offshore. Mailing printed materials

The thrust of Reg S is whether securities have truly "come to rest" abroad.

to U.S. investors or advertisements in U.S. circulated publications are examples of such prohibited activities.

Reg S categorizes issuers in three different groups, subject to different levels of restriction reflecting the likelihood the securities sold will flow back into the United States and the degree of information available to U.S. investors regarding such securities. One of the more contentious restrictions, as adopted, was a so-called "Restricted Period" of 40 days, during which no offers or sales could be made to U.S. persons of the Reg S securities. Such restriction was intended to help show that the Reg S-offered securities had truly "come to rest" abroad, the thrust of Reg S. However, the 40 days instead became a roadmap to issuers for the waiting period necessary before their Reg S securities could be resold in the United States, thereby giving the buyers much sought after liquidity and evading registration requirements.

Abuses were so voluminous that in 1995, the SEC issued a release entitled, "Problematic Practices Under Reg S." While the SEC recognized that Reg S was serving some legitimate uses, too many market participants were purportedly affecting offshore issuances under Reg S, but in fact were really just attempting to skirt the registration requirements under the securities laws. In its release the commission drew attention to a Preliminary Note to Reg S, which stated that the Safe Harbors of Reg S, even if technically complied with, are not available if they are "part of a plan or scheme to evade registration."

The SEC's main concerns included unregistered transactions disguised as Reg S offerings; straightforward Section 5 violations where Reg S is cited as the exemption, but no real attempt to follow the spirit of the regulation is made; and resales of Reg S securities under other provisions and of restricted securities under Reg S. The violations were so onerous, in a later release amending Reg S the SEC stated that the Commission was acting to "stem [the] abuses of Reg S" and has "instituted enforcement proceedings against participants in abusive Reg S transactions."

Too many market participants were purportedly
affecting offshore issuances under Reg S,
but in fact were really just attempting to skirt
the registration requirements
under the U.S. securities laws.

The Loophole Is Shut

In order to stop these abusive practices, the SEC in February 1998 amended Reg S as it related to equity securities issued by domestic companies. Such amendments included changing the restricted period from 40 days to one year (and renaming it "distribution compliance period" so as not to be confused with the holding period for restricted securities). They also classified Reg S issued and resold securities as "restricted securities" under Rule 144, thereby stopping a practice of using Reg S resale provisions to "wash off" the restrictions from restricted securities previously issued pursuant to other exemptions. Moreover, the new and clarifying rules included all equity securities and all securities convertible into equity securities issued by domestic issuers pursuant to Reg S.

While the SEC still touts the advantages of Reg S, the delay in being able to resell the securities into the United States from 40 days to one year significantly reduces the attractiveness of Reg S to many issuers. The effect will likely be more significant for small U.S. issuers, since more seasoned, larger U.S. issuers eligible to register using Form S-3 have ceased relying on Reg S for foreign placements and have instead registered their foreign securities offerings either on the offering or for resale into the United States.

Under Rule 415 shelf registration, an issuer can register any number of securities "to be offered and sold on a continuous basis" at current market value, up to a dollar amount equal to 10 percent of its voting stock's aggregate dollar value, so long as it reasonably expects to sell the securities in the next two years. Issuers may register all such securities in an abbreviated Form S-3 registration statement, so long as the issuer had continuously reported under the '34 Act for at least one year, and had at least a $75 million public float (owned by nonaffiliates) if engaging in a primary offering for cash. The Form S-3 must contain certain information regarding the issuances and any material changes in the issuer's business, but the rest of the required information concerning the issuer is incorporated by reference to past and future '34 Act reports. Thus when an issuer wants to market, or "takedown," a new offering from "off the shelf," it needs only to file an abbreviated prospectus supplement detailing the offering and the securities.

While it can be cost effective to the issuer
to use a shelf registration,
such advantage has to be weighed
against the potential liability imposed upon issuers
by Section 11 of the '33 Act
and the accompanying duty imposed upon
underwriters to exercise due diligence
when using a shelf registration.

Shelf registration offers both advantages and disadvantages to traditional '33 Act Registration. While it can be cost-effective to the issuer, in terms of both the costs of the issuances and of disclosure, such advantage has to be weighed against the potential liability imposed upon issuers by Section 11 of the '33 Act and the accompanying duty imposed upon underwriters to exercise due diligence when using a shelf registration. Since shelf registration transactions can occur extremely quickly, underwriters may not have the opportunity to conduct a sufficient level of due diligence. Moreover, issuers can suffer from an "overhang" from the market, due to the shelf-registered securities awaiting issuance, causing investors to stay away from the issue for fear of future dilution. So, despite shelf registration's promise of an efficient, rapid means of raising capital, certain aspects of this approach way limit the system's usefulness to issuers and investors.

Conclusion

The laws, rules, and regulations related to PIPEs are extensive and intricate. This Appendix is intended to provide a high-level overview of the relavent securities laws, how and why they evolved, and how they may interact. The SEC has stated that more than technical compliance with the laws is necessary. Not adhering to the proper rules and regulations related to private placements, exemptions, safe harbors, potential integration and resales can be a disaster for the issuers, investors, and existing shareholders. Indeed, without a complete understanding of the legal framework of PIPEs, the entire company can be put at risk. Executives are advised that there is no substitute for expert legal advice. Use this information as a foundation for your discussions with your legal advisor regarding the legal issues associated with your PIPE financing.

INDEX

Index